First published in 2005 by
Carlton Books Limited
20 Mortimer Street
London W1T 3JW

Arsenal.com

A CIP catalogue record for this book is available
from the British Library

ISBN 1 84442 561 4

Editorial Manager: Martin Corteel
Project Art Director: Darren Jordan
Design: Ben Ruocco
Picture Research: Tom Wright
Gunnersaurus illustration (pp 52–53): Des Taylor
Production: Lisa French

Printed in Italy

The Publishers would like to thank the following sources for their kind
permission to reproduce the pictures in this book. Location indicator (t-
top, b-bottom, m-middle, l-left, r-right).
Empics: /Matthew Ashton: 41bl, /PA: 27r, 42, /S&G/Alpha: 27m, 27br,
/Neal Simpson: 27tl; **Getty Images:** 36-37, /Laurence Griffiths: 21,
/Clive Mason: 7, /Jamie McDonald: 41mr, /Clive Rose: 48, /Matthew
Rose/Bongarts: 20, /Shaun Botterill: 56

All other Images kindly supplied by Arsenal Football Club:
Photographers **Stuart MacFarlane** & **David Price**

The Official
Arsenal
Annual 2006

Chas Newkey-Burden

CARLTON
BOOKS

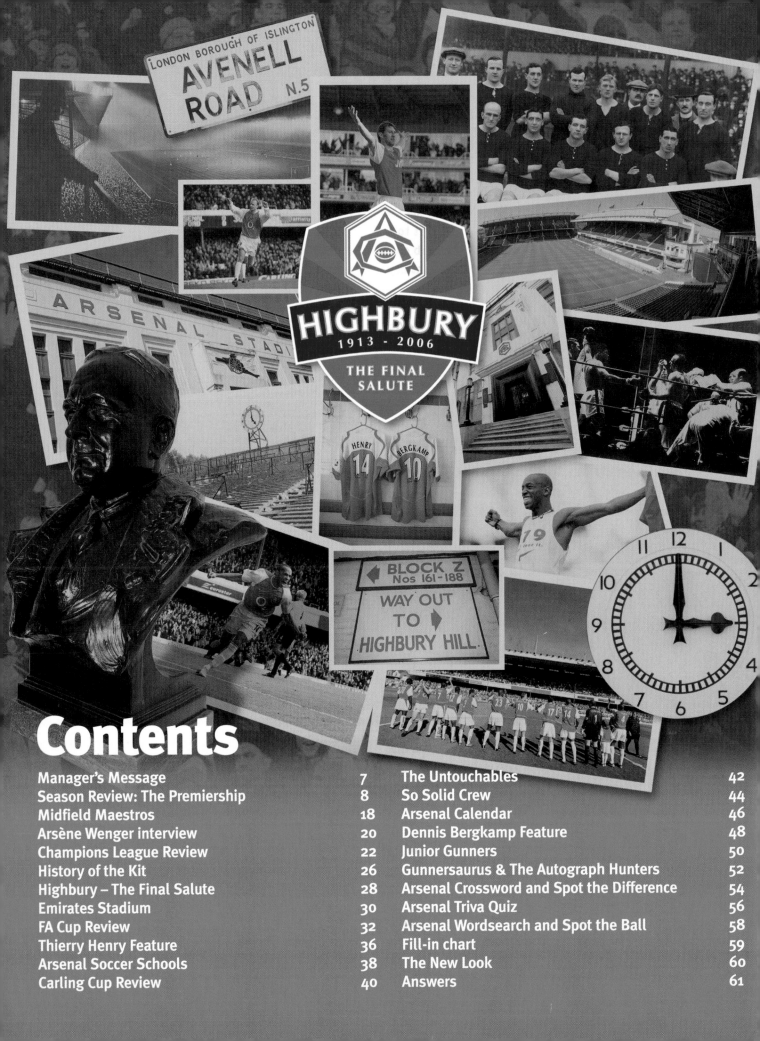

Contents

Dear Supporters,

Welcome to another Official Arsenal Annual. The 2004/05 season was an exciting one and there are many reasons why we should be proud of our team.

We started, and finished, the season with important victories over Manchester United. The first was the 3-1 Community Shield win, where we played very well and gave us a good start to the season. The second was the FA Cup Final win, a victory which gave the Club our tenth FA Cup win in our history and our third in five years. It was a great day in Cardiff and thank you to all the fans who travelled to cheer us on.

In addition, the 2004/05 season saw us set a new record for consecutive unbeaten league games – 49, as well as finishing the season with a Club record amount of Premiership goals – 87. I am particularly proud of the unbeaten record, as it stretched over three seasons and is a sign of the team's remarkable consistency over that time.

There were a number of performances which, for me, highlight the kind of exciting team we have at Arsenal. Our 7-0 victory over Everton at the end of the season, for example, was a fabulous way to end our domestic season at Highbury.

The 2004/05 season also saw the emergence of several young players who I believe will have major parts to play in Arsenal's future. Youngsters like Philippe Senderos, Cesc Fabregas, Gael Clichy and Robin van Persie all have the opportunity to learn from the experienced players in the squad and improve to become regular Arsenal players.

Thank you to all the Arsenal fans who, in 2004/05, cheered the team on. Your support was invaluable and played a huge part in our season.

Many thanks,

Arsène Wenger, Manager

And they're off! Bergy nets the first goal of the campaign

Defending the Premiership title is always an enormous challenge and at the end of a highly competitive league season, Arsenal finished second. The campaign began and ended in blistering fashion and in between there was drama, goals and skill galore! Relax and enjoy some marvellous memories from an incredible season!

AUGUST 2004

The Champions began the season away to Everton and continued in the same fashion that served them well throughout the previous campaign – playing slick, stylish football. Dennis Bergkamp opened the scoring in the 23rd minute and Jose Antonio Reyes made it 2–0 with a header. The second-half saw Freddie Ljungberg and substitute Robert Pires also hit the target to secure a winning start to the campaign, 4–1 the final score.

Cesc Fabregas had become Arsenal's youngest ever player to appear in a Premier League game when he was selected to play at

> **❝I THINK IT IS SOMETHING AMAZING TO LOOK AT THE NUMBER OF GOALS WE SCORED IN THE RECORD 43 GAMES WE HAVE GONE UNBEATEN AND THE NUMBER OF VICTORIES WE HAVE HAD.❞**
>
> **ARSENE WENGER**

Goodison Park and the 17-year-old remained in the side when Middlesbrough visited Highbury a week later. An extraordinary match saw the Gunners go from 1–0 up to 3–1 down before emerging 5–3 victors. Thierry Henry gave Arsenal the lead but three Middlesbrough goals in a 10-minute period either side of half-time shook Highbury. A breathtaking fight back, with goals from Bergkamp, Pires and Reyes, restored Arsenal's lead before Henry scored a second to finish off 'Boro.

Next up at Highbury were Blackburn Rovers and they made Arsenal work their socks off. Following a tight, goalless first-half, Henry converted a Bergkamp cross five minutes into the second period. Fabregas doubled the lead and his fellow Spaniard made it 3–0 to cement the win. The champions took over at the top of the table and, more notably, equalled Nottingham Forest's long-standing record of going 42 consecutive league games unbeaten.

Arsenal were simply awesome at Carrow Road as they swept past Norwich City. Goals from Reyes, Henry and Pires effectively ended the contest by half-time. As the visiting fans chanted "We are unbeatable", Bergkamp added a fourth from the final attack of the afternoon. Arsène Wenger's men had scored 16 goals in four games and gone top of the table – August was a truly unbeatable month.

AUGUST 15, 2004 EVERTON 1–4 ARSENAL
(BERGKAMP 23, REYES 39, LJUNGBERG 54, PIRES 83)
AUGUST 22, 2004 ARSENAL 5–3 MIDDLESBROUGH
(HENRY 26, 90, BERGKAMP 54, PIRES 65, REYES 66)
AUGUST 25, 2004 ARSENAL 3–0 BLACKBURN
(HENRY 50, FABREGAS 58, REYES 79)
AUGUST 28, 2004 NORWICH CITY 1–4 ARSENAL
(REYES 22, HENRY 36, PIRES 40, BERGKAMP 90)

SEPTEMBER 2004

Arsenal extended their unbeaten run to 45 games and collected all three points against a resolute Fulham side at Craven Cottage. An eventful first-half saw both sides have penalty claims rejected and a Fulham "goal" disallowed. The Gunners took control in the second-half as strikes from Ljungberg and Reyes, either side of an own goal from Zat Knight, secured another away win for Arsenal. At the close of their fifth game of the campaign, Arsenal had five wins and Reyes had scored five goals. Equally thrilling for Gunners fans was the sight of Patrick Vieira returning from injury.

An in-form Bolton Wanderers side arrived at Highbury and gave Arsenal quite a game. Despite a superb performance from the home side and goals from Henry and Pires, Wanderers came twice from behind to grab a 2–2 draw. Any disappointment felt that Arsenal had not won the match was eased by the knowledge that they remained top of the table at the end of the afternoon.

Arsène Wenger's team extended its lead at the top of the table to two points with a much-deserved victory away to Manchester City. Ashley Cole's first-half strike – his first goal for ten months – won the points for the visitors and wrapped up another majestic month for the champions.

SEPTEMBER 11, 2004 FULHAM 0–3 ARSENAL
(LJUNGBERG 62, KNIGHT (O.G.) 65, REYES 71)
SEPTEMBER 18, 2004 ARSENAL 2–2 BOLTON WANDERERS
(HENRY 31, PIRES 66)
SEPTEMBER 25, 2004 MANCHESTER CITY 0–1 ARSENAL
(COLE 14)

> **❝I THINK IF YOU LOOK AT OUR RECORD OF SEVEN GAMES WITH JUST TWO POINTS DROPPED, WE CAN BE VERY PLEASED WITH THAT. PATRICK VIEIRA RETURNING WAS VERY POSITIVE ALSO.❞**
>
> **ARSENE WENGER**

> **❝TO GET THE WINNING GOAL AT MANCHESTER CITY WAS GREAT FOR ME. BUT I THINK I CAN GET MUCH BETTER THAN I AM AT THE MOMENT. I THINK I'M DOING OK BUT BY MID-SEASON I SHOULD BE FULLY INTO THE RHYTHM.❞**
>
> **ASHLEY COLE**

The Swedest feeling! Freddie sinks Fulham

Celebration times: (far left) Thierry and Robert against Bolton and (left) Freddie, Thierry and Jose at Fulham

> **"I CONGRATULATE MY PLAYERS. AT THE END OF THE DEFEAT AT OLD TRAFFORD THEY CAME OUT WITH A FANTASTIC RECORD AND SHOWED THEY ARE A GREAT SIDE."**
>
> **ARSENE WENGER**

OCTOBER 2004

Arsenal opened the month by simply sweeping Charlton Athletic aside with an awesome performance. The pick of their four goals was the first of Henry's two strikes, an impudent back-heel three minutes after the interval. Ljungberg and Reyes completed the scoring.

Sol Campbell made his 100th Premiership start for Arsenal and helped the team run out 3–1 winners against Aston Villa. Despite going behind after just three minutes, Arsenal bounced back with two goals from Pires and one from Henry. Extending their unbeaten run to 49 matches, the Gunners played some breathtaking football and dominated possession throughout the afternoon.

After going so long without facing defeat in a league match, Arsenal had to lose eventually and it took a trip to Old Trafford, a determined Manchester United side and an element of misfortune for it to happen. The Gunners dominated the match and did not deserve the 2–0 defeat Manchester United inflicted on them but could be justly proud of their incredible unbeaten record.

> **"ROBIN'S GOAL WAS SENSATIONAL. BUT IT WASN'T A BIG SURPRISE TO SEE ROBIN SCORE A GOAL LIKE THAT BECAUSE WE HAVE SEEN HIM DO IT MANY TIMES IN TRAINING."**
>
> **PATRICK VIEIRA**

Robert is spot on as he converts a penalty against Aston Villa

Back at Highbury, Robin Van Persie's first Premiership goal for Arsenal rescued a point at the end of an action-packed clash with Southampton. Henry slotted home a Bergkamp pass to give Arsenal the lead but two goals from Rory Delap looked set to give the visitors all three points. But in the last minute, Van Persie smashed home a shot from the edge of the area to grab a point and send Highbury into raptures.

OCTOBER 2, 2004 ARSENAL 4–0 CHARLTON ATHLETIC
(LJUNGBERG 33, HENRY 48, 69, REYES 70)
OCTOBER 16, 2004 ARSENAL 3–1 ASTON VILLA
(PIRES 19 (PEN), 72, HENRY 45)
OCTOBER 24, 2004 MANCHESTER UNITED 2–0 ARSENAL
OCTOBER 30, 2004 ARSENAL 2–2 SOUTHAMPTON
(HENRY 67, VAN PERSIE 90)

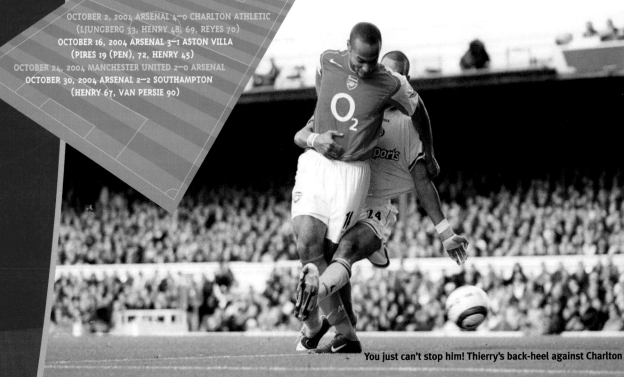

You just can't stop him! Thierry's back-heel against Charlton

Captain fantastic's derby delight as he makes it 3–1

NOVEMBER 2004

A mixed month for Arsenal in the Premiership kicked-off at Selhurst Park. There, the Champions found a determined Crystal Palace side prepared to make a battle of it. Henry gave Arsenal the lead after great work by Fabregas and Ljungberg but two minutes later, Palace were level after Aki Riihilahti broke the offside trap and slotted home.

Next up was another London derby away to Tottenham Hotspur – and a remarkable one at that. At the end of the first-half, the score was 1–1. The second-half was breathtaking and the Gunners were soon 3–1 ahead after Lauren and Vieira had scored. After being pegged back to 3–2, Ljungberg restored the two-goal cushion. Then Spurs grabbed another before Robert Pires made it 5–3. There was still time for another goal from Tottenham to see the match finish 5–4. Extraordinary.

"MY GOAL AGAINST SPURS WAS THE HIGHLIGHT FOR ME BUT I WAS STILL UNHAPPY AT THE GOALS WE CONCEDED. OKAY, WE SCORED FIVE GOALS AWAY BUT WE MUST BE BETTER AT DEFENDING."

LAUREN

West Bromwich Albion arrived at Highbury – complete with Arsenal old boy Kanu – and held the Gunners to a 1–1 draw. The home side dominated possession and took the lead through Pires but a late equaliser salvaged a point for Bryan Robson's men.

The month ended on a disappointing note when Liverpool snatched all three points at Anfield. Patrick Vieira scored a fantastic goal – his first at Anfield – after a powerful run into the box to equalise Liverpool's opener. However, Liverpool grabbed the

Thierry opens the scoring in the draw at Crystal Palace

win in stoppage time after Neil Mellor's spectacular volley beat Lehmann.

NOVEMBER 6, 2004 CRYSTAL PALACE 1–1 ARSENAL
(HENRY 63)
NOVEMBER 13, 2004 TOTTENHAM HOTSPUR 4–5 ARSENAL
(HENRY 45, LAUREN 55 (PEN), VIEIRA 60, LJUNGBERG 69, PIRES 81)
NOVEMBER 20, 2004 WEST BROMWICH ALBION 1–1 ARSENAL
(PIRES 54)
NOVEMBER 28, 2004 LIVERPOOL 2–1 ARSENAL
(VIEIRA 57)

DECEMBER 2004

After some disappointing results in October and November, the Champions were unbeaten in December. Manuel Almunia made his Premiership debut against Birmingham City and kept a clean sheet as Arsenal won 3–0 with goals from Pires and two from Henry including a late header.

The following weekend, league leaders Chelsea came to Highbury in a hugely important match. Arsenal made a fantastic start when a Henry volley gave them the lead in the second minute. Chelsea equalised and Arsenal took the lead once more through Henry. The visitors again clawed a goal back and the game ended 2–2 meaning Chelsea had not beaten Arsenal in the League for 10 seasons.

After two consecutive league games at Highbury, the Gunners took to the road to face Portsmouth. A tight match looked set to be headed for a goalless draw until Sol Campbell strode forward and unleashed a fierce volley that handed all three points to Arsenal.

While households across the country had relatives visiting for the afternoon, Arsenal played host to Fulham on Boxing Day. But far from showering their visitors with gifts, the Gunners stuck two goals past Fulham and sent them on their way. Henry's opener was his 128th league goal for Arsenal, equalling Ian Wright's post-war record. Pires added the second in the second half.

Thierry gives fans a Boxing Day gift as he scores against Fulham

DECEMBER 4, 2004 ARSENAL 3–0 BIRMINGHAM CITY
(PIRES 33, HENRY 80, 86)
DECEMBER 12, 2004 ARSENAL 2–2 CHELSEA
(HENRY 2, 29)
DECEMBER 19, 2004 PORTSMOUTH 0–1 ARSENAL
(CAMPBELL 75)
DECEMBER 26, 2004 ARSENAL 2–0 FULHAM
(HENRY 12, PIRES 71)
DECEMBER 29, 2004 NEWCASTLE UNITED 0–1
ARSENAL (VIEIRA 45)

Sol long Pompey! Campbell scores at Fratton Park

"MY GOAL AGAINST BIRMINGHAM CITY — MY 50TH PREMIERSHIP STRIKE FOR ARSENAL — HELPED RELIEVE A LOT OF TENSION FOR US AS WELL AS THE FANS."

ROBERT PIRES

Arsène Wenger contends that 2004 was one of the best years in Arsenal's illustrious history and his team brought the curtain down on it with a winning performance at St James' Park, Newcastle. Vieira scored the winner in the 45th minute when his 25-yard volley was deflected past Shay Given.

The following weekend Arsenal returned to winning ways at home to Newcastle United. Bergkamp grabbed the winner in the 19th minute when he casually controlled Mathieu Flamini's pass and shot past Shay Given. The Newcastle United goalkeeper went on to enjoy a fantastic performance and single-handedly prevented a massacre. This match completed a league double against Graeme Souness's team.

Kolo leads Gary Speed a merry dance

JANUARY 1, 2005 CHARLTON ATHLETIC 1–3 ARSENAL
(LJUNGBERG 35, 48, VAN PERSIE 71)
JANUARY 4, 2005 ARSENAL 1–1 MANCHESTER CITY
(LJUNGBERG 75)
JANUARY 15, 2005 BOLTON WANDERERS 1–0 ARSENAL
JANUARY 23, 2005 ARSENAL 1–0 NEWCASTLE UNITED
(BERGKAMP 19)

JANUARY 2005

Arsenal kicked off the New Year by beating Charlton Athletic 3–1 after a tough, physical match. Two goals from Ljungberg and one from Van Persie gave the Gunners the points and meant they had not been beaten for 32 London derbies.

The team was unable to keep its winning run going when Manchester City rolled up at Highbury. Shaun Wright-Phillips gave City the lead in the first-half and it was only a Ljungberg strike 15 minutes from time that saved Arsenal from losing. Van Persie hit the bar late on and the Gunners had to settle for a point.

Arsène Wenger's side have often found it hard to win at the Reebok Stadium and so it proved again in January. Despite enjoying superior possession and a better shots-on-target tally, the Gunners went down 1–0 leaving them with a mountain to climb to retain their Championship.

Twist and shout! Robin on target again

FEBRUARY 2005

A month of highs and lows began with a bitterly disappointing night at Highbury. Manchester United were the visitors and despite Arsenal taking the lead twice through Vieira and then Bergkamp, Sir Alex Ferguson's men ended the match 4–2 victors. It was one of those bad nights that make Arsenal fans enjoy the good times even more.

> **❝THE SEASON IS NOT OVER FOR US, WE HAVE MUCH TO PLAY FOR AND I AM FOCUSSED ON GIVING MY BEST SO WE CAN FINISH IN THE STRONGEST POSITION POSSIBLE.❞**
>
> **JOSE ANTONIO REYES**

The Gunners needed to bounce back at Villa Park and they did so in style. Freddie Ljungberg gave Arsenal a tenth-minute lead and they went on to dominate the match. Four minutes later, Henry made it 2–0 and then Cole wrapped the game up with his superb 28th-minute strike. Perhaps as impressive though was Arsenal's overall dominance and style. The football of champions indeed.

Seven great minutes in the first-half of Arsenal's home match against Crystal Palace tied up the game for the Gunners. Bergkamp, Reyes and Henry all scored during those seven minutes and Vieira added a fourth in the second half. Henry made it five for Arsenal in the 77th minute to cap one of the finest performances from Arsenal for some time.

The month ended on a less positive note when Arsenal threw away a half-time lead at Southampton and emerged with just a point. Ljungberg made it 1–0 on the stroke of half-time, just after the Saints had been reduced to 10 men. Sadly, Arsenal also lost a man in the second-half when Robin Van Persie was sent off and they also conceded a goal. The visitors pressed for a winner but were unable to find one.

> **❝DON'T FORGET THAT IF YOU LOOK AT THE LEAGUE WE HAVE SCORED MORE GOALS THAN EVERYBODY ELSE. REYES LOOKS CONFIDENT AGAIN, HE HAD A GREAT GAME AGAINST CRYSTAL PALACE.❞**
>
> **ARSENE WENGER**

The Palace keeper can't bear to look as Patrick walks the ball into the net

Kneesy does it!
Ash celebrates at Villa

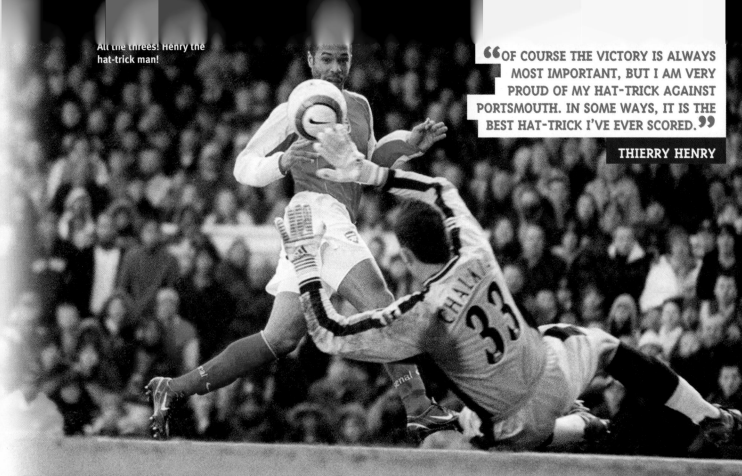

All the threes! Henry the hat-trick man!

March 2005

The Gunners had just two Premiership games in March, but they impressed in both. First, Portsmouth arrived at Highbury and were swept aside in style thanks to a magnificent hat-trick from Henry, his sixth for Arsenal. Henry's first goal came when he converted a cross from Lauren; his second came after a fine pass from Vieira helped him outpace defenders; the third came when Kostas Chalkias failed to stop a Henry free-kick.

The match was notable also for a fine performance by the back-four who kept a clean sheet in Pascal Cygan's 50th league appearance for Arsenal.

"WE'LL DO AS WELL AS WE CAN OF COURSE TO COME BACK. WE WANT TO FINISH AT LEAST SECOND AND AS CLOSE AS POSSIBLE TO CHELSEA, AND WE'LL FIGHT TO THE END TO DO THAT."

ARSENE WENGER

There was another clean sheet for Arsenal at Blackburn Rovers. The clash was inevitably billed as a dress rehearsal for the forthcoming FA Cup semi-final but both sides were focussed on the three points up for grabs.

MARCH 5, 2005 ARSENAL 3–0 PORTSMOUTH
(HENRY 39, 53, 85)
MARCH 19, 2005 BLACKBURN ROVERS 0–1 ARSENAL
(VAN PERSIE 43)

Robin Reliable! Van Persie scores the only goal at Ewood Park

Arsenal took all the points home with them thanks to a fine goal from Van Persie after the young Dutchman jinked his way through the home defence just before the half-time interval.

Perhaps the most satisfying factor in the victory at Ewood Park was that it was secured despite the Gunners being hit by injuries. Henry, Edu, Campbell, Bergkamp, Pires and – at the last moment – Ljungberg were all missing. It is testimony to the hard work of Arsène Wenger that he can still put out a winning side despite so many absentees.

HENRY'S HAT-TRICK SINKS POMPEY...SHEETS STAY CLEAN...ROBIN ROCKS ROVERS...

15

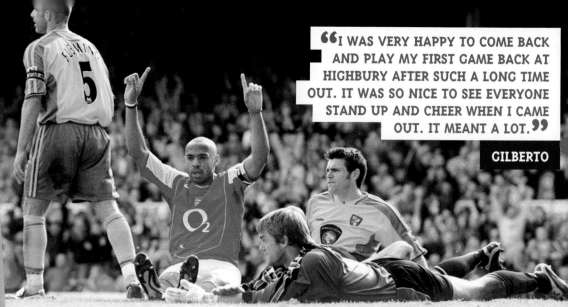

"I WAS VERY HAPPY TO COME BACK AND PLAY MY FIRST GAME BACK AT HIGHBURY AFTER SUCH A LONG TIME OUT. IT WAS SO NICE TO SEE EVERYONE STAND UP AND CHEER WHEN I CAME OUT. IT MEANT A LOT."

GILBERTO

It's so threesy! Thierry claims the match ball

APRIL 2005

Another unbeaten month in the Premiership for the Gunners began with a cracking victory over Norwich City inspired by Thierry Henry's hat-trick. Henry's seventh hat-trick in Arsenal colours was also the second consecutive home league match in which he had scored three times. The match was also notable for the return of Gilberto who made his first appearance for the Gunners since September 18, 2004. Freddie Ljungberg grabbed the fourth goal of the afternoon.

That goal fest was followed by a hard-fought 1–0 victory at the Riverside Stadium. Robert Pires scored in the 73rd minute and a cracking team effort – personified by an impressive performance by Jens Lehmann – ensured that his goal was enough to complete a fourth consecutive league double over Middlesbrough.

Then it was time for the top two to meet at Stamford Bridge. A tight but entertaining match ended 0–0 meaning the Gunners had avoided defeat in both of their matches against the eventual champions.

"FOR A WHILE WE HAD ONE OF THE WORST DEFENSIVE RECORDS BUT THAT HAS IMPROVED RECENTLY. IT WAS EASY TO SCORE IN THE AIR AGAINST US BUT THAT IS NOT THE CASE ANYMORE. WE ARE TALLER AND MUCH MORE SECURE ON SET PIECES."

ARSENE WENGER

The game was played in fine spirit and the respect between both sets of players and coaching teams was evident at the final whistle.

The month ended with a 1–0 victory over local rivals Tottenham Hotspur. Jose Antonio Reyes scored the winning goal midway through the first half after some fantastic work by Cesc Fabregas. Again, the Gunners kept it tight and held onto their lead to complete their first league double over Tottenham for 16 years.

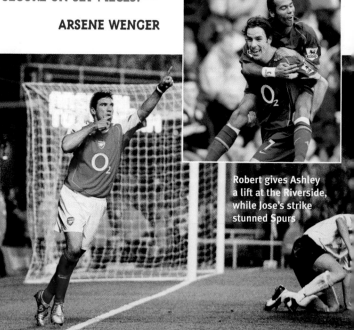

Robert gives Ashley a lift at the Riverside, while Jose's strike stunned Spurs

APRIL 2, 2005 ARSENAL 4–1 NORWICH CITY
(HENRY 19, 22, 66, LJUNGBERG, 50)
APRIL 9, 2005 MIDDLESBROUGH 0–1 ARSENAL
(PIRES 73)
APRIL 20, 2005 CHELSEA 0–0 ARSENAL
APRIL 25, 2005 ARSENAL 1–0 TOTTENHAM HOTSPUR
(REYES 22)

May 2005

May was a memorable month in the Premiership for Arsenal. Scoring 13 goals in just four matches, the Gunners were firing on all cylinders. At The Hawthorns, Arsenal had to work hard against a West Bromwich Albion side that was fighting against relegation, but second-half goals from Robin Van Persie and Edu secured a 2–0 Arsenal victory.

It was all back to Highbury for Arsène Wenger's men as the team prepared for the visit of Liverpool.

Again, Arsenal's opponents had special reason to seek the points: in this case Liverpool were fighting to secure Champions' League football for the following season. Robert Pires and Jose Antonio Reyes were both on target in the first-half and even though Steven Gerrard pulled one back, Arsenal ensured the points when the great Cesc Fabregas got number three in the final minute.

Next up at Highbury were the other Merseyside team and Everton must have wished they hadn't bothered

as Arsenal thumped them 7–0 in an extraordinary match. Van Persie, Vieira, Edu and Flamini all scored and Pires netted twice. However, the biggest cheer came for Dennis Bergkamp's goal as the Dutchman had been the architect of much of the evening's entertainment.

Bergkamp was on target again at St Andrews on the final day

of the Premiership campaign. However, Birmingham City's Emile Heskey scored on the final whistle to secure a 2–1 victory for the home side. A mildly disappointing conclusion to an accomplished Premiership campaign for Arsenal.

MAY 2, 2005 WEST BROMWICH ALBION 0–2 ARSENAL
(VAN PERSIE 66, EDU 90)
MAY 8, 2005 ARSENAL 3–1 LIVERPOOL
(PIRES 25, REYES 29, FABREGAS 90)
MAY 11, 2005 ARSENAL 7–0 EVERTON
(VAN PERSIE 8, PIRES 12 50, VIEIRA 37, EDU 70 (PEN), BERGKAMP 77, FLAMINI 85)
MAY 15, 2005 BIRMINGHAM CITY 2–1 ARSENAL
(BERGKAMP 88)

> **IT WAS A GREAT PERFORMANCE AGAINST EVERTON BECAUSE THERE WAS ALWAYS SOMETHING SHARP GOING ON, SOME FANTASTIC TOUCHES ON THE PITCH. I'M A LITTLE BIT ENVIOUS BECAUSE I WOULD LIKE TO BE IN THE MIDDLE OF ALL THAT.**
>
> **ARSENE WENGER**

Plucky seven! Dennis delights against Everton

Robin breaks the West Brom deadlock (above) while Cesc celebrates a birthday goal against Liverpool

> **AGAINST LIVERPOOL, I FELT REALLY COMFORTABLE ON THE PITCH. I'VE ALWAYS WANTED TO WIN A MAN-OF-THE-MATCH AWARD IN THE PREMIER LEAGUE, TO ME IT IS A TROPHY. IT WAS ONE OF THE BEST PRESENTS I COULD GET FOR MY 18TH BIRTHDAY!**
>
> **CESC FABREGAS**

Meet the men in the middle!

They are the men who patrol the central pastures of pitch. Protecting the back four, dominating the midfield and helping create attacks – life is busy for our central midfielders. There are now four top-quality players vying for the two positions in the centre of midfield. How much do you know about them? It's time to meet the men in the middle!

PATRICK VIEIRA

Date Of Birth: 23 June 1976
Previous clubs: Cannes, AC Milan
Signed for Arsenal: 14 August 1996

Strengths
An absolute colossus on the field, Patrick's strengths are his engine and his dominance. How many other players in Europe can break up attacks and drive their team-mates on as well as the Arsenal captain?

Greatest Arsenal moment
His opening goal at White Hart Lane in the game that won the Gunners the 2004 Premiership title.

Did you know?
Although Patrick was one of Arsène Wenger's first signings for Arsenal, he arrived at Highbury a month before Mr Wenger took charge of his first match.

CESC FABREGAS

Date Of Birth: 4 May 1987
Previous clubs: Barcelona
Signed for Arsenal: 11 September 2003

Strengths
Cesc is one of the quickest thinkers in the Premiership and his speed of mind is perfect for the pacey players around him. Making his debut at just 16, Cesc plays with a maturity that belies his years and also has a great eye for goal. Imagine how good he'll be when he's in his twenties!

Greatest Arsenal moment
The superb control and finish as he scored against Rosenborg in Arsenal's 5–1 Champions League victory in December 2004.

Did you know?
Cesc was top scorer and player of the tournament in the 2003 FIFA Under-17 World Championship.

GILBERTO

Date Of Birth: 7 October 1976
Previous clubs: Atletico Mineiro
Signed for Arsenal: 7 August 2002

Strengths

Good luck to any opposition player trying to create an attack when Gilberto is around – the Brazilian is one of the most effective players in the business at breaking up attacks! He also adds a great aerial presence to the team and has weighed in with some important goals for the Gunners.

Greatest Arsenal moment

His fine goal and match-winning performance in the 4–1 victory at Leeds United in the 2004 title-winning season.

Did you know?

Gilberto played with a broken back for two months at the start of the 2004/05 season.

MATHIEU FLAMINI

Date Of Birth: 7 March 1984
Previous clubs: Marseille
Signed for Arsenal: 22 July 2004

Strengths

Brimful of energy and stamina, Mathieu is a genuine all-round midfield ace. He can play in the centre or on the right of midfield and has been compared by his manager to former Gunners ace Ray Parlour. His surging, attacking runs into the box have already see him claim assists for many goals. There seems little doubt there are plenty more where they came from!

Greatest Arsenal moment

His dominant performance and fine assist in Arsenal's 1–0 victory over Newcastle United in January 2005.

Did you know?

Mathieu says if he hadn't made it as a footballer he would have trained to be a lawyer!

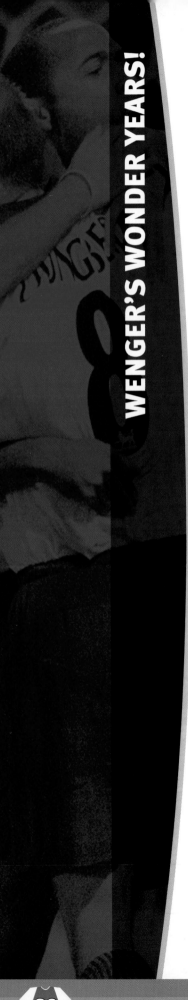

Arsène talks about his Highbury years

Arsène Wenger has been Arsenal manager for nine years. During his glorious reign, the Club has won a host of trophies including three Premiership titles and four FA Cups, he has signed and developed some of the planet's leading footballers and also received a gong from the Queen! Here, Mr Wenger looks back on a hugely successful period for the club...

Mr Wenger, what were your first impressions of the Club when you arrived in 1996?

"Of course I was already very aware of Arsenal and I knew it was a big club. But I was surprised that there was such a big interest in the Club in the country among supporters and the press. On the field, I immediately saw that there was something special about the team. They had a good camaraderie because they have been playing together for a long time. So I had to adapt because I didn't want to destroy what the strong point of Arsenal was."

The team won the Double in your first full season. How proud did that make you?

"That was then my greatest achievement as a manager and I was proud for the Club, my staff, the players and the supporters. We showed tremendous spirit all season and our last goal against Everton, on the day we won the Premiership, typified that as Steve Bould sent Adams through. The difference between that Double year and the previous season was that in the Double year, we won the matches against the top Premiership teams. I was surprised but delighted that we won the title so soon."

The team won the Double again in 2002, which of the two Doubles are you prouder of?

"I believe the 2002 Double was an even greater achievement because we were frustrated at the end of the previous season and we showed great character to bounce back. Also, I think it was more difficult to win the FA Cup in 2002 than 1998 because we played bigger teams. And our overall record from 2002 was even stronger than four years earlier. Not only did we win the Championship – we won it in style. To win 14 games away from home and draw the other five is immense. We also scored in every game, which shows we always approach matches in an attacking way."

Winning the Championship is always a real achievement, so how special was it to win it without losing a single league game, as the team did in 2004?

"It was the biggest moment since I've been here … I'm very happy and proud of the players. I always dreamt that we could win the Championship without losing a single league match. This one was the most satisfying of the three titles I have won since I joined Arsenal. I have the greatest respect for championship winners, to go out there each week and keep winning shows great character. The team has not only exceptional talent but it has something more – what players add themselves."

What about the future?

"My life is so closely linked with this Club now that it's so difficult for me to imagine not being at Arsenal. I feel I've been here my whole life. I've been at different clubs before, and I spent a long time at Monaco and Grampus Eight, but I've never had this feeling before. I love this Club and am very happy here. My desire is to take this Club forward and fulfil my ambitions. I still have so much to achieve. I want to maintain and build on our success. The Champions League is our next challenge and I believe we have the quality in the squad to win it one day. These are exciting times for Arsenal and I'm proud to be the manager."

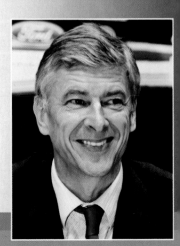

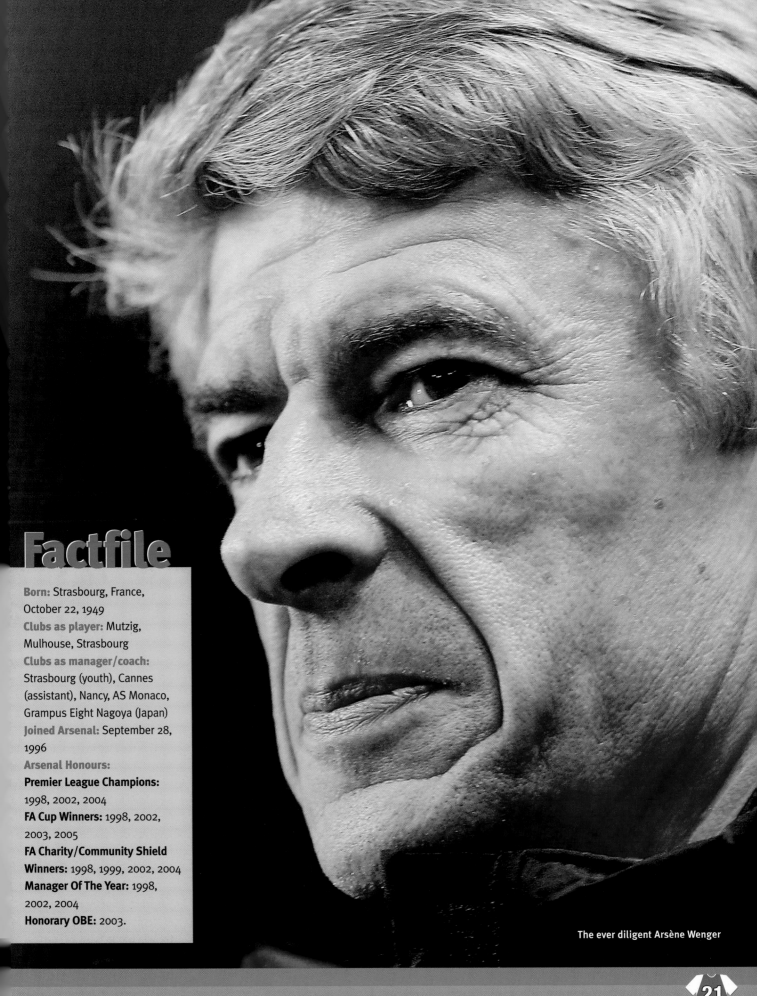

Factfile

Born: Strasbourg, France, October 22, 1949

Clubs as player: Mutzig, Mulhouse, Strasbourg

Clubs as manager/coach: Strasbourg (youth), Cannes (assistant), Nancy, AS Monaco, Grampus Eight Nagoya (Japan)

Joined Arsenal: September 28, 1996

Arsenal Honours:

Premier League Champions: 1998, 2002, 2004

FA Cup Winners: 1998, 2002, 2003, 2005

FA Charity/Community Shield Winners: 1998, 1999, 2002, 2004

Manager Of The Year: 1998, 2002, 2004

Honorary OBE: 2003.

The ever diligent Arsène Wenger

A packed house! The Gunners go 1-0 up against PSV

Freddie celebrates his goal in Greece

Arsenal lost only one of their eight UEFA Champions League games. Although the campaign ended in disappointment, there were many great performances along the way and many happy memories to take from the campaign. First up, came the group stages and the Gunners finished top of the pile in Group E.

GROUP STAGE
home v PSV (Matchday 1)

The Gunners got their Euro campaign off to a winning start thanks to an own goal from PSV defender Alex. The victory came, however, thanks to a focussed, hard-working performance from an Arsenal side determined to do well in this season's competition. Top of Group E, this was a fine start to the Champions League effort.

Euro fact: This was Arsenal's first home victory over Dutch opposition for 34 years.

away v Rosenborg (Matchday 2)

Arsenal continued their unbeaten run in the Champions League as they took to the Euro road for the first time in the competition. Freddie Ljungberg opened the scoring in the sixth minute, tapping home from a Thierry Henry corner. Although Rosenborg equalised in the second-half, the Gunners remained top of Group E at the end of the night.

Euro fact: This was the tenth consecutive Champions League tie that Arsenal had scored in.

away v Panathinaikos (Matchday 3)

Arsenal twice took the lead in Greece but had to settle for a point at the end of a hard-fought European encounter. Ljungberg gave the visitors the lead in the 17th minute with a fine chip after a superb pass from Jose Antonio Reyes. The Greeks equalised in the 65th minute but a fantastic counter-attacking move from Arsenal saw Henry make it 2–1 nine minutes later. A late Panathinaikos goal made it 2–2.

Euro fact: After three matches, Arsenal were the only unbeaten team in Group E.

Cesc Appeal! Fabregas nets v Rosenborg

Thierry netted in all of the last four Group E games

home v Panathinaikos (Matchday 4)

Days after missing a penalty against Southampton, Henry showed his professionalism and nerve by converting a spot-kick in the 16th minute. The Gunners deserved their lead and both Henry and Reyes had chances to double it. However, a 30-yard strike from Loukas Vintra deflected off Pascal Cygan to again deny Arsenal a victory.

Euro fact: Thierry Henry has scored four goals in three games against Panathinaikos.

away v PSV (Matchday 5)

Arsenal made an awful start when Andre Ooijer gave PSV the lead after eight minutes. But the Gunners showed their never-say-die spirit and maintained their unbeaten Champions League run thanks to a fine goal from Henry. He scored after some great interplay with Ljungberg. Even when Arsenal were reduced to nine men in the second-half, they denied PSV victory.

Euro fact: Henry's goal left him 20 short of the all-time Gunners scoring record.

home v Rosenborg (Matchday 6)

When Reyes opened the scoring in the third minute, he became one of five Arsenal players to score on a must-win night at Highbury. Henry was next up to score on 24 minutes and Highbury erupted five minutes later when a fantastic volley put Cesc Fabregas on the score-sheet. Four minutes before half-time Robert Pires scored from the spot and then six minutes from full-time, Robin Van Persie made it five for Arsenal.

Euro fact: Cesc Fabregas and Robin Van Persie's goals were their first in the Champions League for Arsenal.

EURO STATS

SEPTEMBER 14, 2004, ARSENAL 1–0 PSV EINDHOVEN (ALEX (O.G.) 42)
SEPTEMBER 29, 2004, ROSENBORG 1–1 ARSENAL (LJUNGBERG 6)
OCTOBER 20, 2004, PANATHINAIKOS 2–2 ARSENAL (LJUNGBERG 17, HENRY 74)
NOVEMBER 2, 2004, ARSENAL 1–1 PANATHINAIKOS (HENRY 16 (PEN))
NOVEMBER 24, 2004, PSV EINDHOVEN 1–1 ARSENAL (HENRY 31)
DECEMBER 7, 2004, ARSENAL 5–1 ROSENBORG (REYES 3, HENRY 24, FABREGAS 29, PIRES 41 (PEN), VAN PERSIE 84)

GROUP E FINAL STANDINGS

	P	W	D	L	F	A	PTS
ARSENAL	6	2	4	0	11	6	10
PSV EINDHOVEN	6	3	1	2	6	7	10
PANATHINAIKOS	6	2	3	1	11	8	9
ROSENBORG	6	0	2	4	6	13	2

Drawn against German giants Bayern Munich, Arsenal faced a stiff task to progress through to the quarter-finals. Although the Germans ultimately got the better of the Gunners winning 3-2 on aggregate, Arsène Wenger's men will return in the competition for the 2005–06 season and will never lose their determination.

KNOCK-OUT STAGES AND MEMORIES

A late strike from Kolo Toure underlined Arsenal's never-say-die spirit once again and threw a lifeline to Arsène Wenger's men for the second-leg of this tie. However, there was no denying the damage done by Bayern's three goals in this, the only match Arsenal were to lose in Europe all season.

Euro fact: Bayern won the European Cup three years in succession during the 1970s.

Brave at Bayern:
Patrick keeps fighting

A tense night at Highbury's saw Arsenal put in a brave, determined performance ending in victory against one of Europe's finest sides. But it was still not enough to keep them in the competition. Henry's fine goal on 66 minutes separated the sides but there was no hiding the team's disappointment at the final whistle. They'll be back.

Euro fact: Henry's goal put him level with Cliff Bastin as Arsenal's second highest goalscorer in history.

Henry's goal against Bayern at Highbury was not enough

EURO STATS

FEBRUARY 22, 2005, BAYERN MUNICH 3–1 ARSENAL (TOURE 90)
MARCH 9, 2005, ARSENAL 1–0 BAYERN MUNICH (HENRY 66)

Edu and Toure celebrate in Italy

There is nothing quite like a great performance in European competition. The tension among all fans knowing what is at stake, the unfamiliar opponents and stadiums. Since Arsène Wenger arrived at Highbury in 1996, his team has been involved in some classic European nights at Highbury and at grounds around Europe. So sit back and enjoy reliving memories of some classic European matches from Arsène's time and before.

MIGHTY EURO MATCHES!

Celta Vigo 2–3 Arsenal
(Edu 2, Pires)
24 February, 2004
(UEFA Champions League)

This was Arsenal's first victory in Spain in the Champions League and what a way to secure it! Edu scored twice and Robert Pires made the win safe after Celta had fought their way back into the game.

Inter Milan 1–5 Arsenal
(Ljungberg, Henry 2, Edu, Pires)
25 November, 2003
(UEFA Champions League)

One of the greatest nights in Arsenal's history saw Freddie Ljungberg, Edu, Pires all find the net and Thierry Henry score twice. The Gunners showed their true class and absolutely routed the Italian giants on their own turf.

AS Roma 1–3 Arsenal (Henry 3)
27 November, 2002
(UEFA Champions League)

This was Thierry Henry's night as the attacking genius, ably assisted by his team-mates, grabbed a glorious hat-trick with goals in the 6th, 70th and 75th minutes. It could have been so different because the Gunners had fallen behind in just the fourth minute. The pick of Henry's goals was his third, a cracking free-kick.

Freddie strikes in Holland

Miracle in Milan: Thierry scores against Internazionale

PSV Eindhoven 0–4 Arsenal
(Gilberto, Ljungberg 2, Henry)
25 September, 2002
(UEFA Champions League)

The Gunners got off to a dream start in Holland when Gilberto netted in the first minute. In the second-half, goals from Ljungberg and two from Henry completed a most satisfying scoreline.

Lens 1–2 Arsenal (Henry, Kanu)
20 April 2000 (Uefa Cup)

Leading 1–0 from the first-leg of this semi-final, the Gunners booked their place in the Uefa Cup final with a cracking performance in northern France. A goal in each half from Henry and Kanu guaranteed their place in the final in Copenhagen.

Barcelona 1–1 Arsenal (Kanu)
29 September 1999
(UEFA Champions League)

An injury-struck Arsenal side were not given much of a chance of anything but defeat in this tie at the Nou Camp but thanks to a goal from Kanu nine minutes from time, they walked out with a hard-earned but throroughly deserved point.

Parma 0–1 Arsenal (Smith)
4 May 1994 (Cup Winners' Cup)

Alan Smith's 20-yard first-half shot was enough for Arsenal to see off Italians Parma in the Cup Winners' Cup final in Copenhagen.

Back To The Future!

For the final season at Highbury, the Arsenal players will be kitted out in a commemorative kit that recalls the team's first season at the ground and takes in the most up-to-date features to help the boys perform at their best. Inspired by the very first kit worn at the ground in 1913, it is "redcurrant" and recreates and reflects the origins of the unique stadium. Find out all about the new kit and discover what Arsène Wenger and his players think about it.

A TEAM EFFORT

The decision to return to the 1913 design involved many people. The designers at Nike, manager Arsène Wenger and Gunners supporters who attend the regular fan forums with the Club. Members of Arsène Wenger's backroom staff were also involved in the technological discussions, especially kit manager Vic Akers. Everyone agreed that it was important the kit commemorated Highbury in the final season there. The Arsenal players all looked at the early prototypes and absolutely loved the idea!

NO SWEAT!

The main colours of the shirt and shorts are very similar to the 1913 design. However, 93 years of technological advancements mean there are key differences to the 1913 version which will benefit the players. The old shirts were made of wool so thick that when there was heavy rainfall, players said they felt as if they were playing in deep-sea diving suits! Patrick Vieira and his team-mates will face no such problems. This shirt is made from a stretch woven lightweight fabric, with extra stretch panels on the sleeves and collar to provide comfort and freedom of movement. Mesh vent sections have been placed in key areas to help prevent heat build up and all the seams are flat to prevent chafing and aid

"PERSONALLY, I LOVE THE FACT THAT THE TEAM WILL BE WEARING A HOME KIT THAT IS INSPIRED BY THE FIRST ONE EVER WORN AT HIGHBURY. IT'S NOT ONLY A WAY OF ENCAPSULATING MORE THAN 90 YEARS OF MEMORIES, IT ALSO TAKES US RIGHT BACK TO WHEN WE STARTED AT THIS GROUND IN 1913. "

ARSENE WENGER

comfort. The socks and shirts now have a DWR (Durable Water Repellency) to help prevent the material absorbing sweat or rain. So come rain or shine, the Gunners players will be perfectly kitted out!

HOME AFFAIRS

The theme of the home kit has rarely changed in design since Herbert Chapman introduced white sleeves to the shirt during the 1930s. For the 1965–66 season, when the team was having a tough time and it was felt that they needed something to break the cycle and lift the burden of the club's great history, the red and white shirt was replaced by an all-red version, with just a touch of white on the collar. However, the team continued to struggle and so the kit clearly wasn't the problem. The following season, the

traditional kit returned. When Arsenal kick-off the 2006/07 season at Emirates Stadium, the Club will again revert to a red kit with traditional all-white sleeves.

AWAY

The Arsenal players have already turned out in a kit that is a modern take on a traditional design. The recent yellow away shirt was very popular as many people felt it was a nod to the shirt worn in that famous 1971 FA Cup Final. The fact that Arsenal never lost an FA Premier League game in that kit helped its popularity too! Similarly, the away shirt of the 1991–92 season had its detractors in the press who said the chevron print design resembled tractor tyre tracks or an out-of-focus TV screen! However, thousands and thousands of these shirts were sold, perhaps in part because it was worn during the winning FA and League Cup runs of the 1992/93 season.

"I THINK IT IS FANTASTIC WE WILL BE WEARING A COMMEMORATIVE KIT THAT REPRESENTS THE HISTORY OF THIS MAGNIFICENT STADIUM. I THINK THAT GOING BACK TO THE KIT FROM 1913 IS A REALLY NICE TOUCH. "

PATRICK VIEIRA

HIGHBURY 1913 — 2006
THE ORIGINAL KIT BACK FOR ONE LAST TIME · 22ND JUNE

"I THINK THE KIT IS GREAT. IT'S BACK TO THE ROOTS, BACK TO WHAT THE FIRST KIT WAS LIKE. I LIKE THE FACT THAT IT'S TRADITIONAL AND IT IS EXACTLY HOW IT WAS AT THE BEGINNING OF HIGHBURY."

THIERRY HENRY

The 2005/06 season is Arsenal's final campaign at Highbury. As the club prepares to launch a series of special events to give the ground a final salute, take a look at some fantastic facts about the home of football...

HIGHBURY
1913 - 2006
THE FINAL SALUTE

THE EARLY DAYS

The site originally belonged to St John's College Of Divinity. It consisted largely of two football pitches, two cricket pitches and a tennis court used by students. Arsenal payed £20,000 for a 21-year lease.

Although known as Highbury, the correct name for our current home is Arsenal Stadium.

The new pitch had to be levelled because the north end was 11 feet too low and the south end five feet too high.

The first match played at Highbury was against Leicester Fosse on 6 September 1913. The club was still then known as Woolwich Arsenal at this point, they won 2–1.

During that match, centre-forward George Jobey sprained his ankle. There were no dressing rooms, or running water, at the ground so for treatment he was taken to the players' lodgings on a milkman's cart!

The banks that the supporters first stood on were made of the soil left over from the digging of Gillespie Road Underground station, which had opened seven years previously.

During the 1932/33 season, manager Herbert Chapman got the local Gillespie Road Underground station renamed 'Arsenal'.

The West Stand was opened on 10 December 1932 by the then Prince Of Wales.

Architect Claude Ferrier designed the West Stand. A bust of Ferrier resides in the West Stand executive lounge.

The East Stand, designed by William Birnie, was rebuilt in 1936.

The North Stand was originally called the Laundry End.

THE WAR YEARS

During the Second World War, Arsenal played their home matches at Tottenham because Highbury was commandeered as an Air Raid Precautions site.

The North Bank roof caught fire during the War when a bomb set fire to piles of bunk beds being stored in the stadium.

In 1940, *The Arsenal Stadium Mystery*, a murder mystery movie set in the ground, was released.

THE MODERN ERA AND BEYOND...

The new North Stand was opened in August 1993.

Later in the 1993/94 season, the Clock End became all-seater for the first time.

The East and West Stand facades, together with the marbles halls and other key elements of Highbury will be retained when redevelopment of the site commences following Arsenal's move in 2006 as they are Grade II listed buildings.

The pitch will be retained and converted into a formal garden square.

Supporters will be able to revisit their old home when a new footpath route is created and opened to members of the public.

THE FIN

A Team Effort!

We all know that Arsenal will move to a new home for the 2006–07 season. But how much do you know about the building of the Club's new citadel? Find out how Arsenal players, managers, directors and fans have all had a part to play in a true team effort!

FANS FOR THE MEMORIES!

Arsenal fans have played their own part in the character of the new stadium. Thousands of supporters voted to decide what objects should be placed in the Time Capsule that will be placed at the Emirates Stadium site. The objects include: a list of all Arsenal players, a piece of Highbury turf, a picture of a crowded North Bank, a stadium flag used at Highbury and a signed photo of Gunnersaurus.

PLAYERS PARTICIPATE!

Patrick Vieira and Thierry Henry are among the Arsenal players who have visited the stadium site many times to check on the latest progress. They were also present to place the Time Capsule in the new stadium!

YOUNG FANS PLAY IT SAFE!

Young Arsenal supporters have also played a part in making the construction of the new stadium a success. Arsenal teamed up with RoSPA (The Royal Society For The Prevention Of Accidents) and local newspaper the *Highbury & Islington Express*, to launch a campaign encouraging local children to design "Play Safe" posters to display on hoardings at the new stadium. Steven Kourtellis, aged 13, won the 12–16 years category and ten-year-old Robert Hayden won the 11-and-under category.

ARSÈNE KNOWS!

The Training Centre, opened in 1999, was built to Arsène Wenger's specifications and the Arsenal manager has had a huge input into the new stadium. He has had particularly close involvement in plans for the dressing rooms and the players' bench. He says: "I've been involved in every aspect of the players' facilities at Emirates Stadium and am involved in regular update meetings. Just one example of a new facility for players at the new stadium is that we will have water facilities in the

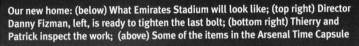

Our new home: (below) What Emirates Stadium will look like; (top right) Director Danny Fizman, left, is ready to tighten the last bolt; (bottom right) Thierry and Patrick inspect the work; (above) Some of the items in the Arsenal Time Capsule

dressing rooms, which will include a little pool and a massage pool."

A NEW DIRECTION!

Director of Arsenal Football Club Danny Fizman also had a hand in the building of the stadium –

quite literally! Danny helped connect two halves of the first main truss at the Stadium. In full safety gear, Danny was lifted up to the platform on the temporary support tower to tighten the last of the many bolts holding the huge truss together.

Did you know?

The lowdown on our new home!

• The overall project cost is £357 million.

• It is anticipated that 1,140,000 supporters will attend Premiership matches at the new 60,000-capacity stadium in one season.

• Marble similar to that which famously decorates the East Stand entrance at Highbury will be used in entrances at the Club's new home.

• A revolutionary Arsenal Seat will take supporter comfort to a new level at Emirates Stadium. The upholstered seat will have integrally fitted pads, as well as

a higher back and a larger seat area than in any other stadium in the UK. Sitting comfortably? You will be!

• The sponsorship agreement with Emirates Airlines was worth £100 million. It gave the airline naming rights to Arsenal's new stadium for 15 years and made them Arsenal's shirt sponsor for eight years starting from the 2006/07 season – the Club's first at the new stadium.

• You can see live footage of the new stadium via a webcam at arsenal.com

Cup Kings!

To say Arsenal love the FA Cup would be an understatement. The Club has won the competition 10 times, reaching the final a record-equalling 17 times. The 2004/05 season saw the team reach the Final for the fourth time in five years and beat Manchester United in a gripping Final. Here is your chance to relive another winning campaign.

THIRD ROUND – JANUARY 9, 2005
ARSENAL 2–1 STOKE CITY
(REYES 50, VAN PERSIE 70)

FOURTH ROUND – JANUARY 29, 2005
ARSENAL 2–0 WOLVERHAMPTON WANDERERS
(VIEIRA 53 (PEN), LJUNGBERG 82)

home v Stoke City (Rd 3)

Wayne Thomas rocked Highbury with the opening goal just before half-time but a fine comeback saw Arsenal book their place in the fourth round. Kolo Toure crossed for Jose Antonio Reyes to score five minutes after the break. Then, with 20 minutes left, Robin Van Persie got the winner.

Match fact: Emmanuel Eboue made his Arsenal first-team debut in this tie.

home v Wolves (Rd 4)

The Gunners made it into the Fifth Round at the end of a one-sided cup tie at Highbury. Patrick Vieira scored from the penalty spot in an interesting foreshadow of the Final and Freddie Ljungberg made the win safe eight minutes from time. In truth, Arsenal could have won by many more had the visiting goalkeeper not been in such inspired form.

Match fact: This was the third time Arsenal faced Wolves in the FA Cup under Wenger's reign. The Gunners have won all three ties.

> **"WE NEEDED OF COURSE TO PLAY OF COURSE WITH A HIGHER TEMPO IN THE SECOND HALF TO GET ON TOP OF THE GAME, AND ONCE THE SECOND GOAL CAME IN, IT LOOKED ALWAYS LIKE WE COULD SCORE EVERY MINUTE."**
>
> **ARSENE WENGER**

Patrick's penalty power! The skipper nets against Wolverhampton Wanderers

Manuel's the man! Almunia makes sharp saves against the Blades

home v Sheffield United (Rd 5)

An eventful tie ended all-square following a sending off, a last-minute penalty and drama galore. The Gunners had Dennis Bergkamp sent off after 35 minutes but when Robert Pires gave the home team the lead with 12 minutes to go, it looked like Arsenal were through. With 20 seconds left, however, United forced a replay when Andy Gray converted a penalty.

Match fact: Manuel Almunia made his FA Cup debut in this tie.

away v Sheffield United (Rd 5 replay)

Both teams could have won the tie in 90 minutes with Cesc Fabregas and Freddie Ljungberg going close for the visitors. Then, in the dying seconds of normal time, Jon Harley was denied by a spectacular save from Manuel Almunia.

Ultimately it went to penalties. Lauren, Vieira, Ljungberg and Cole were all on target for Arsenal, so Almunia ensured victory with two excellent saves.

away v Bolton Wanderers (Rd 6)

An eventful opening saw Arsenal go 1–0 ahead and the home team reduced to 10 men in the first eight minutes. Freddie Ljungberg was the happy scorer of the goal, while

WE NEEDED A LOT OF CHARACTER AND IF WE HAD NOT SHOWN STRENGTH, RESILIENCE AND DETERMINATION WE WOULD HAVE GONE OUT TODAY.

ARSENE WENGER

El-Hadji Diouf was the less happy recipient of the red card. Both sides had numerous chances, but Arsenal bravely held out for their fifth successive FA Cup semi-final.

Match fact: Lauren made his 200th appearance for Arsenal in this tie.

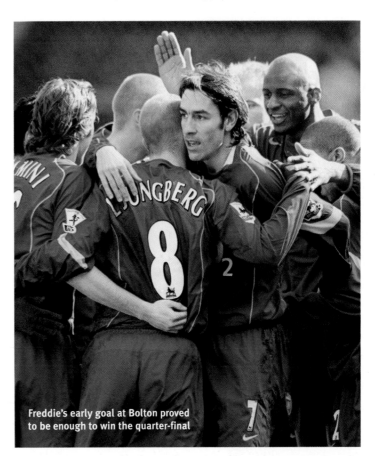

Freddie's early goal at Bolton proved to be enough to win the quarter-final

FIFTH ROUND – FEBRUARY 19, 2005
ARSENAL 1–1 SHEFFIELD UNITED
(PIRES 78)

FIFTH ROUND REPLAY – MARCH 1, 2005
SHEFFIELD UNITED 0–0 ARSENAL
(AET ARSENAL WIN 4–2 ON PENALTIES)

QUARTER-FINAL – MARCH 12, 2005
BOLTON WANDERERS 0–1 ARSENAL
(LJUNGBERG 3)

Robert opens the
semi-final scoring

"I'M VERY HAPPY BECAUSE HAVE SHOWED GREAT CONSISTENCY. WE HAVE BEATEN A TOUGH TEAM."

ARSENE WENGER

Right Van man! Robin rejoices against the Rovers

N v Blackburn (sf, at Cardiff)
Arsenal's record 25th FA Cup semi-final appearance ended with glorious victory. Doubters had been circling around Arsenal before the game against Blackburn, a side that proved to be very tough to beat, especially with Thierry Henry out injured.

Rovers did indeed start well but the Gunners took the lead shortly before the break when Robert Pires tapped the ball home following great work from Kolo Toure. However, the star of the day was substitute Robin Van Persie, who only joined the action with just seven minutes left, but still managed to score twice to make the victory safe.

With Manchester United beating Newcastle United in the other semi-final, an epic Final was set up. United had twice beaten Arsenal in the Premiership this season and ended their Carling Cup campaign.

Match fact: Arsenal are only the second club ever to appear in five consecutive FA Cup semi-finals; they have won four of these.

SEMI-FINAL – APRIL 16, 2005
(MILLENNIUM STADIUM, CARDIFF)
ARSENAL 3–0 BLACKBURN ROVERS
(PIRES 42, VAN PERSIE 86, 90)

FINAL – MAY 21, 2005
(MILLENNIUM STADIUM, CARDIFF)
ARSENAL 0–0 MANCHESTER UNITED
(AET ARSENAL WON 5-4 ON PENALTIES)

Could the Gunners have the "Final laugh" when they returned to the Millennium Stadium in May?

N v Man Utd (final, at Cardiff)

For a second successive season, Patrick Vieira lifted a major trophy and made history in doing so. Last year, it was the Premiership trophy after an unbeaten season, this time it was the FA Cup after winning the first ever Final decided by a penalty shoot-out.

Although Arsenal were perhaps second-best for large periods of the match, they showed their true resilience and character to come through the 90 minutes and extra-time and take the match to penalties. For all Arsenal fans, victory in the FA Cup over Manchester United tastes sweet however it is achieved.

This time, it was achieved through a shoot-out that Arsenal negotiated perfectly. After Ruud van Nistelrooy had converted the opening kick and Lauren matched him, Jens Lehmann saved excellently to deny Paul Scholes. Freddie Ljungberg, Cristiano Ronaldo, Robin Van Persie, Wayne

Rooney and Ashley Cole all scored but, after Roy Keane succeeded with the last of United's five spot-kicks, Vieira scored his to win the FA Cup for Arsenal and spark wild celebrations.

It was fitting that Lehmann and Vieira were the key figures in the shoot-out as they had been

Arsenal's best players throughout the match. The team then stepped up to receive the trophy and celebrate with their fans. Another victory for the Cup Kings!

Match fact: Arsenal have appeared in four of the five FA Cup Finals played in Cardiff during Wembley's rebuilding, and they have won three times.

Teams

Arsenal: Lehmann, Lauren, Toure, Senderos, Cole, Fabregas (Van Persie 86), Vieira, Gilberto, Pires (Edu 105), Bergkamp (Ljungberg 65), Reyes. Unused subs: Almunia, Campbell.
Man Utd: Carroll, Brown, Ferdinand, Silvestre, O'Shea (Fortune 77), Fletcher (Giggs 91), Keane, Scholes, Ronaldo, van Nistelrooy, Rooney. Unused subs: Howard, G Neville, Smith.
Attendance: 71,876.
Referee: Rob Styles.

Jens makes the vital save ...

...And Patrick wins the Cup

❝I'M VERY PROUD BECAUSE IT WAS A DIFFICULT GAME. WE REALLY HAD TO DIG DEEP.❞

ARSENE WENGER

The Cup that cheers! Patrick enjoys the Gunners' tenth FA Cup final victory

Speaking Up!

On the field, Thierry Henry exudes determination and purpose and the same qualities are evident in the anti-racism campaign he has launched. Some of the biggest names in the game joined Thierry to launch the Stand Up Speak Up campaign to encourage football fans across the planet to challenge racism. You may have noticed players and fans across Europe wearing the interlocked black and white wristbands which are the symbol of the campaign. Here, Thierry discusses the origins and successes of the initiative...

What inspired you to launch the campaign, Thierry?

"Lots of people were coming up to me and asking my feelings, my reaction to what [Spain coach] Luis Aragones had said to Jose Antonio Reyes about me. All I could answer was that I don't actually have any power to do or say anything. Okay, I can talk in the Press but what is that going to do? Then I thought why don't all the recognised players in the game try to get together and get behind a campaign where we can send a message and fight against racism?"

Were you partly inspired by black footballers of the past and the hard times they endured?

"Most definitely. I remember when I was at school and our English teacher brought in a book that we had to translate. It was about John Barnes suffering racism in the UK and I saw that picture of him on the pitch and

the banana that was thrown at him. People like him suffered even more than us but they still played well, still won trophies and they fought against it. "

In the past, campaigns have tended to focus on the fans but yours also includes the players...

"Well at the end of the day, we are the ones involved in it. Don't get me wrong, I know that if there are no fans there is no game,

but we are the ones playing and I believe suffering the most. I know the wristband idea is fashionable at the moment and also I thought we could make an advert."

But you also want the fans to take a stand, don't you?

"Yes, we are sending a message out to the fans, making them aware of what is going on and telling them that we need to erase this from football. What can I do on the pitch? I can't shout back at someone who abuses me because I'd get a red card and a three-game ban. So the campaign is all about telling the fans that the players need them. Okay, we can do back-heels, we can do this and that on the pitch, but some things are out of our control."

Speaking out! Thierry Henry tackles racism

Are any other players involved?

"Yes, we've got many including Rio Ferdinand, Roberto Carlos, Claude Makelele and Ronaldinho. We have to get the message through to the next generation of fans so hopefully if kids hear Ronaldinho saying something then it means more to them than if a politician says it."

What happens to the money made from the sales of the wristbands?

"It goes to the King Badouin Foundation in Belgium who have done a lot of work against racism. They then distribute the money to different campaigns that are challenging racism, such as Let's Kick Racism Out Of Football."

Are you optimistic that the campaign will be a success?

"Yes, I am sure it will be. I just feel that at the moment when you talk about football you talk about racism and I don't want that to be the case in the sport I love. We all love the game, the fans, the players, so let's all fight together."

Community Spirit!

Arsenal FC is a community club and you will find no better evidence of that than the enormously successful Arsenal Soccer Schools. Here, boys and girls of all ages and abilities are given the chance to improve their football skills in a fun and safe environment. Some 13,000 youngsters attended an Arsenal Soccer School last year.

Memories are made of this! Coaches and players line up for a group photo with the Premiership trophy

How long have the Soccer Schools being going?

The Arsenal Soccer Schools have been in existence for 20 years and have expanded from the Sports Centre at Highbury to more than 100 venues across more than a dozen countries!

Who can come along to the Soccer Schools?

They are open to boys and girls of all abilities so the playing standard of children attending is mixed. The more talented players are developed by being moved to more advanced sessions and ultimately onto the Arsenal Academy!

What activities go on at the Schools?

They work on a modular system of training, designed to progressively improve all-round ability. This includes warm up, stretching and reaction games. Coaching and development sessions cover all aspects and techniques needed in a game of football. Sessions include: passing, control, dribbling, running with the ball; heading, shooting, attacking and defending; small-sided matches and tournaments. There is also a daily skills competition. The emphasis is on fun and safety as well as football improvement.

Where do the Tricks 'N' Flicks series fit in?

Tricks has developed into its own module – with the emphasis on beating your opponent and feeling comfortable with a football. The moves include ball-juggling as well as dribbling and control skills. There are Tricks 'N' Flicks lessons in the Arsenal FC matchday programme and monthly *Arsenal* magazine.

Do any of the current first-team stars play a role at the Arsenal Soccer Schools?

When free, first-team Arsenal stars often attend Soccer Schools. Recent players to attend include Patrick Vieira, Thierry Henry, Ashley Cole, Kolo Toure, Dennis Bergkamp, Stuart Taylor, and others. They are delighted to help out and enjoy their involvement as much as the children do!

Have the Schools had any success stories?

Yes and the number one success story is Ashley Cole! Other professionals to come through the doors include Ryan Smith and Paolo Vernazza. Ellen Maggs – a striker for the Arsenal Women's team – is also a Soccer Schools graduate. The Soccer Schools coaching staff work with the Arsenal Academy coaches to develop young talent. A number of players in the current Arsenal Academy came through the Soccer School route. Watch out for them in the future! However, the Soccer Schools are not just about finding new talent for the team, just as important is that they provide opportunities for youngsters to play football and be associated with Arsenal.

Back to the Future! Ashley Cole first got his hands on a League trophy at an Arsenal Soccer School

"Tricks 'N' Flicks" help players get comfortable on the ball

Youngsters have a ball at the Arsenal Soccer School

Patrick takes a coaching course

To find out more information on Arsenal Soccer Schools, ring 020 7704 4140 or email soccerschools@arsenal.co.uk

Arsenal's 2004/05 Carling Cup campaign ended earlier than hoped, but there were many, many positives to be taken from it. A youthful Arsenal side beat near full-strength teams put out by Manchester City and Everton. The young guns also gave a strong Manchester United side a run for their money. Here, we take a look back at the matches and profile five of the key Arsenal youngsters who came of age during the Carling campaign...

Young Guns star in Carling Cup!

away v Man City (Rd 3)

There were plenty of milestones against an almost first choice Manchester City side. Six Arsenal players made first-team debuts: Manuel Almunia, Sebastian Larsson, Philippe Senderos, Johan Djourou, Daniel Karbassiyoon and Arturo Lupoli. Lupoli and Senderos became the first Italian and first Swiss, respectively, to appear for the Gunners, while Karbassiyoon's 90th minute goal made him the first American to score for Arsenal. City pulled a goal back in stoppage time, but it was an historic night and a great victory!

home v Everton (Rd 4)

Everton were flying high in the Premiership when they arrived at Highbury and fielded a full-strength side. Arsène Wenger kept faith with the young players that had beaten Manchester City – the average age of the Arsenal team was just 19. So when Everton went ahead in the eighth minute, many thought Arsenal were out of the competition. Instead, the Gunners fought back and grabbed the win!

away v Man Utd (Rd 5)

Despite the disappointment felt at Arsenal's exit from the Carling Cup there were plenty of positives to take from this tie. The young guns gave a far more experienced United line-up a real test. Sir Alex Ferguson fielded a strong side including eight full internationals. Going behind in the first minute, the youthful Arsenal side could have capitulated. Robin Van Persie was particularly impressive and this tie offered Gunners fans a glimpse into a positive future for the Club – as did the whole Carling Cup campaign!

Here's to the future! The Arsenal youngsters celebrate against Everton

OCTOBER 27, 2004 – THIRD ROUND
MANCHESTER CITY 1–2 ARSENAL
(VAN PERSIE 78, KARBASSIYOON 90)
NOVEMBER, 9, 2004 – FOURTH ROUND
ARSENAL 3–1 EVERTON
(OWUSU-ABEYIE 25, LUPOLI 52, 85)
DECEMBER 1, 2004 – FIFTH ROUND
MANCHESTER UNITED 1–0 ARSENAL

Five Stars!

During the 2003/2004 season, Cesc Fabregas made his first-team debut in the League Cup and is now a first-team regular. In 2004/05, many new faces appeared during the Carling Cup campaign. Some of them have already followed in Cesc's footsteps and forced their way into the first-team for Premiership and Champions League matches, others are not far behind. Here are five of the best!

ROBIN VAN PERSIE

Position: Striker

Although just 21, Robin was actually one of Arsenal's most experienced players in the Carling Cup run. The former Feyenoord player is a thunderous performer on the pitch and has become a regular player and goal-scorer for the first team.

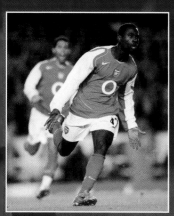

QUINCY OWUSU-ABEYIE

Position: Striker

Joining Arsenal as a scholar from Ajax – where Dennis Bergkamp learnt his trade – Quincy scored his first goal for the Gunners against Everton in the Carling Cup. He has since appeared in the Champions League and Premiership, helping Thierry Henry to his hat-trick at home to Portsmouth.

JUSTIN HOYTE

Position: Defender

Justin is one of the most promising English youngsters to emerge from the Arsenal youth ranks for some time. Another Carling Cup ever-present, Justin's pace and cool head have seen him picked for Premiership and European matches.

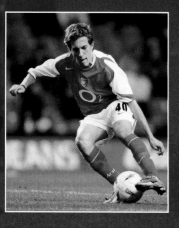

ARTURO LUPOLI

Position: Striker

He joined the Gunners from Parma in July 2004. He appeared in all three of Arsenal's Carling Cup games. He has been capped for Italy at Under-16, Under-17 and Under-19 levels.

PHILIPPE SENDEROS

Postion: Defender

Phillipe was a star performer throughout the Carling Cup campaign. The Swiss defender graduated to appearances for the first-team in the Premiership and FA Cup where he has played with characteristic assurance.

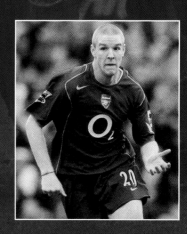

The Unbeaten Run...

Arsenal made history when they went 49 league matches unbeaten and also earned themselves a new nickname - The 49ers! Take a look back at this incredible run and feast your eyes on other key facts and figures from the 2004/2005 season!

Arsenal's 49 match unbeaten run if the fifth longest such run in European football history.

The run began on Wednesday May 7 2003 with a 6-1 defeat of Southampton.

Arsenal used 33 different players during the unbeaten league sequence.

Robert rounds off a winning start to 2004/05

Arsène Wenger's team scored 112 goals and conceded just 35 during the run.

The Gunners amassed 121 points during the 49 matches.

Some 36 of the games were victories, 13 were draws. 15 different players scored during the 49 games.

Thierry Henry scored 39 times, Robert Pires found the back of the net 23 times during the 49 games.

Five own goals were included among the 112 goals Arsenal scored during the run.

Thierry Henry missed just one game, as did Kolo Toure.

Jens Lehmann kept the most clean sheets by a Premiership goalkeeper during 2003/2004.

Ashley Cole and Thierry Henry both were in the uefa.com users' team of the year for 2004.

The previous Arsenal Club record was 30 unbeaten Premiership matches between December 18 2001 and October 19 2002.

Arsenal were presented with a unique replica of the Premiership trophy to commemorate the 2003/2004 unbeaten season.

Arsenal were held to four goalless draws in the 49-game run.

Robert's rocket! Pires was on target when the 49-game run began

...and 2004/2005

— THE REST OF THE INCREDIBLE STORY!

Cesc Fabregas became the youngest Arsenal player to appear in the Premiership when he started the 4-1 victory over Everton on the opening day.

Robin Van Persie became the 100th Premiership player to appear for Arsenal when he made a substitute appearance away

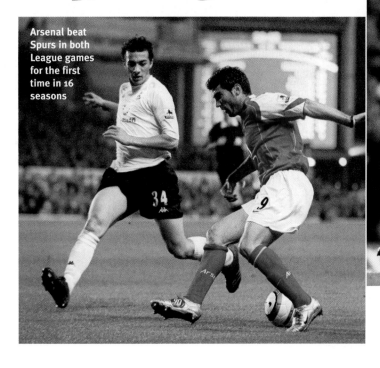

Arsenal beat Spurs in both League games for the first time in 16 seasons

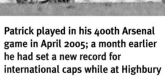

Patrick played in his 400th Arsenal game in April 2005; a month earlier he had set a new record for international caps while at Highbury

to Manchester City in September. The victory in that match was Arsenal's 250th in the Premiership.

Robert Pires scored his 50th league goal for Arsenal against Birmingham City in December 2004.

The Club's home match against Charlton Athletic was Arsenal's 4,000th league match.

The 2004/2005 season saw Arsenal complete their first league double over Tottenham Hotspur for 16 years.

Thierry Henry scored his seventh Arsenal hat-trick against Norwich City in April 2005. This was also the second successive season that he had scored hat-tricks in successive home league matches.

Patrick Vieira became Arsenal's most capped player when he

played in France's 0-0 draw with Switzerland in March 2005.

In April, Patrick made his 400th appearance for Arsenal against Chelsea. He has made the most appearances of the current squad.

Arsenal played their 500th Premiership match away to Middlesbrough on April 9. Robert Pires' winner was Arsenal's 100th goal of the season.

What a screamer! (left) Thierry celebrates another goal; (right) The hat-trick man has Canaries defenders in a flap at Highbury

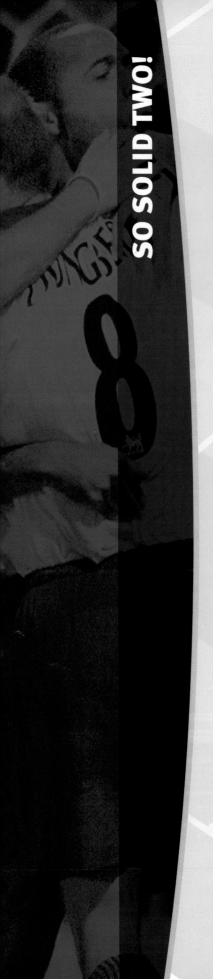

The case for the defence

One of them is 30 years old and 6ft 2in, the other is 24 years old and 5ft 10in; between them, they form a rock at the heart of the Arsenal defence. Sol Campbell and Kolo Toure are the most accomplished central defensive partnership in the Premiership and the pair that helped guide the Gunners to their 49-match unbeaten run.

SOL CAMPBELL

Date of birth: 18 September 1974
Previous club: Tottenham Hotspur

The lowdown

Anyone who wondered how Arsenal would cope following the retirement of the legendary Tony Adams need not have worried – Sol Campbell has been as solid as a rock! The defensive giant is an immense talent: a strong tackler, powerful and pacy.

Sol is also a national hero thanks to his consistently impressive performances for England. He was named in the Euro 2004 all-star squad after some fine performances in Portugal. Watch out for him in the 2006 World Cup!

Defining moment of 2004–05

His winning goal away to Portsmouth. To cap another solid performance in defence, guiding Arsenal to another clean sheet, Sol surged forward in the 75th minute and unleashed a thunderous shot to win another three points for the Gunners.

> **"SOL'S ABILITY AND RECORD SPEAKS FOR ITSELF. HE WAS A VERY TALENTED PLAYER WHEN WE BOUGHT HIM TO THE CLUB AND HE HAS IMPROVED SINCE THEN. HE HAS A QUICK MIND AND MAKES GOOD DECISIONS DURING MATCHES. HE IS VERY IMPORTANT TO US."**
>
> **ARSENE WENGER**

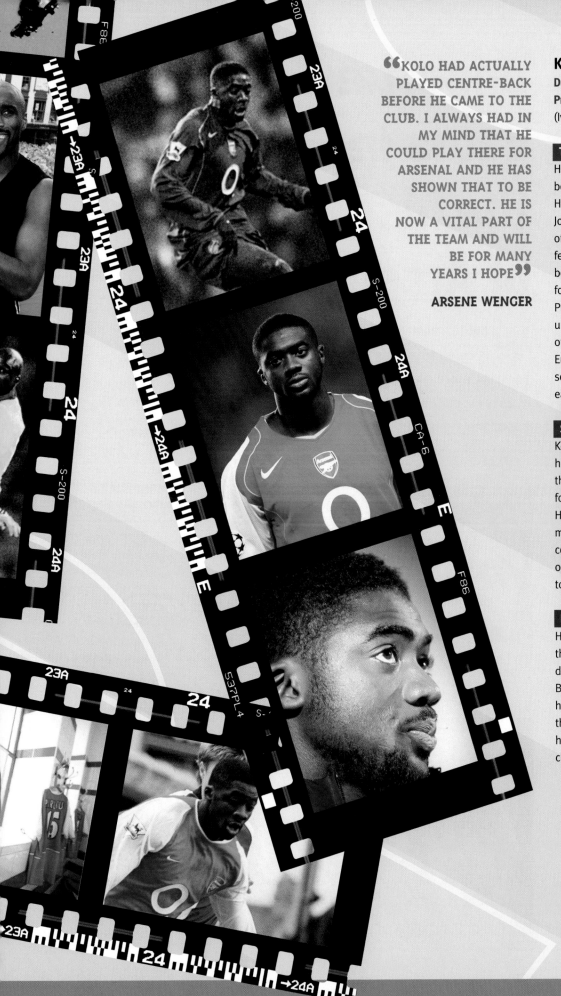

"KOLO HAD ACTUALLY PLAYED CENTRE-BACK BEFORE HE CAME TO THE CLUB. I ALWAYS HAD IN MY MIND THAT HE COULD PLAY THERE FOR ARSENAL AND HE HAS SHOWN THAT TO BE CORRECT. HE IS NOW A VITAL PART OF THE TEAM AND WILL BE FOR MANY YEARS I HOPE"

ARSENE WENGER

KOLO TOURE

Date Of Birth: 19 March 1981
Previous club: ASEC Mimosas (Ivory Coast)

The lowdown:

How many youngsters have become crowd favourites at Highbury as quickly as Kolo did? Joining the Club towards the end of the 2001/02 season, he made a few appearances in midfield before being moved to centre-back for the 2003/04 campaign. One Premiership title and a 49-match unbeaten run later and he is one of the finest centre-backs in Europe and proved throughout his second season in defence that his early success was no fluke.

Strengths

Kolo's energy and enthusiasm are his most admirable qualities for the Highbury faithful but let's not forget what a gifted talent he is. His sense of timing in the tackle is magnificent and he is very comfortable bringing the ball out of defence. He gets the odd goal too!

Defining moment of 2004–05

His goal against Bayern Munich at the Olympiastadion. Although disappointed at his role in Bayern's first goal, Kolo kept his head up and scored himself late in the game to give the Gunners hope for the second-leg. True character.

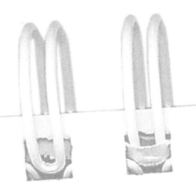

Important dates in the history of Arsenal

Want to know when your favourite player is celebrating his birthday? Fancy knowing more about key anniversaries and events in Arsenal's history? Discover more about the significance to all Gunners fans of days throughout the year...

JANUARY
8th: Arsenal and Tottenham Hotspur met in the FA Cup for the first time. The Gunners won 3–0. (1949)
19th: Lauren is born in Londi Kribi, Cameroon. (1977)
29th: Robert Pires is born in Reims, France. (1973)

FEBRUARY
11th: Royal Arsenal leave their first home, Plumstead Common, and move to the Manor Ground. (1888)
14th: Philippe Senderos (bottom right) is born in Geneva, Switzerland. (1985)
25th: Arsène Wenger buys Nicolas Anelka from Paris St Germain. (1997)

MARCH
6th: Arsenal recorded the biggest ever North London derby win, triumphing 6–0 away to Tottenham Hotspur. (1935)
7th: Mathieu Flamini (bottom left) is born in Marseille, France. (1984)
9th: Arsenal attract their biggest ever attendance at Highbury, with some 73,295 people coming to see them take on Sunderland. (1935)
19th: Kolo Toure is born in Abidjan, Ivory Coast. (1981)

APRIL
3rd: "Woolwich" is officially dropped from the club's name – we become "The Arsenal"! (191_
4th: Tony Adams' header wins th_ FA Cup semi-final against rivals Tottenham Hotspur. (1993)

WHEN DO THESE BOYS CELEBRATE THEIR BIRTHDAYS? FIND OUT HERE!

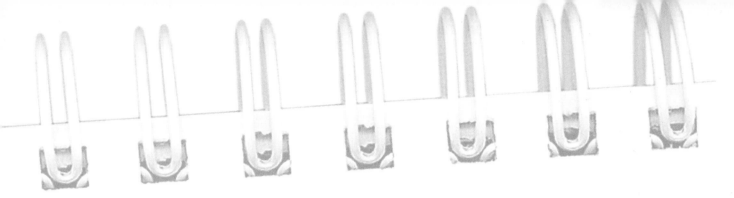

16th: Freddie Ljungberg (middle) is born in Halmstad, Sweden. (1977)

25th: Patrick Vieira and Robert Pires score the goals that sees Arsenal clinch the Premiership title at White Hart Lane. (2004)

28th: Arsenal win the Uefa Cup, beating Anderlecht 3–0 at Highbury (4–3 on aggregate) in the Final. (1970)

MAY

4th: A goal from Alan Smith sees the Gunners beat Parma 1–0 to win the European Cup Winners' Cup. (1994)

8th: Arsenal beat Manchester United 1–0 at Old Trafford to secure the Premiership title and indeed the Double! (2002)

11th: Arsenal record their biggest victory under Arsène Wenger, crushing fourth-placed Everton 7–0 at Highbury. (2005)

15th: Arsenal beat Leicester City 2–1 at Highbury and become the first team since Preston North End in 1888/89 not to lose a League game in a season. (2004)

16th: Arsenal beat Newcastle United 2–0 to win the FA Cup and secure their first double under Arsène Wenger. (1998)

20th: Arsenal beat Sheffield Wednesday 2–1 to win the FA Cup and become the first team to win both the FA Cup and League Cup in the same season. (1993).

26th: A last minute goal from Michael Thomas sees Arsenal clinch the league title at Anfield, beating Liverpool 2–0. (1989)

JUNE

4th: Emmanuel Eboue is born in Abidjan, Ivory Coast. (1983)

14th: Arsène Wenger receives an honorary OBE. (2003)

17th: In an astonishing triple swoop, Arsenal sign Emmanuel Petit, Marc Overmars and Gilles Grimandi. (1997)

20th: Dennis Bergkamp signs for Arsenal (1995).

23rd: Patrick Vieira is born in Dakar, Senegal. (1976)

JULY

1st: Cesc Fabregas joins Arsenal from Spanish giants Barcelona. (2003)

3rd: Sol Campbell signs for Arsenal. (2001)

12th: France beat Brazil 3–0 in the World Cup Final with a squad including past and present Gunners stars Patrick Vieira, Emmanuel Petit, Thierry Henry and Robert Pires. (1998)

25th: Jens Lehmann signs for Arsenal. (2003)

26th: Gael Clichy is born in Paris, France. (1985)

AUGUST

3rd: Thierry Henry signs for Arsenal from Italian giants Juventus. (1999)

6th: Robin van Persie is born in Rotterdam, Holland. (1983)

17th: Thierry Henry is born in Paris, France. (1977)

22nd: Arsenal's match at Anfield is the first game ever to be shown on *Match Of The Day.* (1964).

25th: Arsenal play Sheffield Wednesday in the first football league match to feature players wearing numbers on the backs of their shirts. The home team wore 1–11, the away one wore 12–22. (1928)

29th: Legendary manager Herbert Chapman takes charge of Arsenal for the first time, against Tottenham Hotspur. (1925)

SEPTEMBER

11th: Arsène Wenger buys Swedish midfielder Freddie Ljungberg from Halmstads. (1998)

13th: Ian Wright becomes Arsenal's all-time leading goalscorer with a hat-trick at home to Bolton Wanderers. (1997)

18th: Sol Campbell is born in Newham. (1974)

22nd: Arsène Wenger is born in Strasbourg, France. (1949)

OCTOBER

7th: Gilberto (right) is born in Lagoa da Prata, Brazil. (1976)

10th: Arsenal legends Tony Adams (in Romford, 1966) and Charlie George (in Glasgow, 1950) were born on this day.

12th: Arsène Wenger takes charge of his first game, the 2–0 victory away to Blackburn Rovers. (1996)

30th: The Arsenal Museum opens. (1993)

NOVEMBER

3rd: Arsenal legend Ian Wright is born in Woolwich. (1963)

5th: Gillespie Road tube station officially has its name changed to Arsenal. (1932)

9th: A late header from David Platt secures a 3–2 win over Manchester United en route to the Premiership title. (1997)

20th: Justin Hoyte is born in Waltham Forest, London. (1984)

25th: Arsenal wallop Inter Milan 5–1 at the San Siro. (2003)

DECEMBER

2nd: Cesc Fabregas becomes Arsenal's youngest ever scorer when he nets in the 5–1 League Cup victory over Wolverhampton Wanderers. (2003)

11th: Dial Square – who eventually will become Arsenal – play their first ever match, beating Eastern Wanderers 6–0. (1886)

14th: Ted Drake scores all seven goals as Arsenal beat Aston Villa 7–1. (1935)

26th: Thierry Henry nets his first ever Arsenal hat-trick against Leicester City at Highbury. (2000)

Ice Cool!

Dennis Bergkamp has now completed 10 glorious seasons with Arsenal. In that time, Dennis has wowed us with his skill, taken our breath away with his goals and helped us win numerous trophies. Here, he looks back over his 10 years at Arsenal and....

Factfile

Born: Amsterdam, Holland, May 10, 1969

Former clubs: Ajax, Internazionale

Joined Arsenal: June 20, 1995

Arsenal Honours:

Premier League Champions: 1998, 2002, 2004

FA Cup Winners: 2002, 2003, 2005

FA Charity/Community Shield Winners: 1998, 1999, 2002, 2004

FWA Footballer Of The Year: 1998

PFA Player Of The Year: 1998

International Honours:

National team: 79 games, 37 goals (Dutch record goalscorer)

European Cup Winners' Cup: 1987 (Ajax)

Uefa Cup: 1992 (Ajax), 1994 (Inter)

Looking back to the summer of 1995, what made you want to join Arsenal?

"Well, I had been a big fan of English football since I holidayed in this country as a child. I can remember driving past the big stadiums. In 1995, I was already aware of the great runs the team had had in Europe in the two years before I signed. Then, when Arsenal approached me, I was very impressed by the plans the Club had in terms of playing style and so on. They were also keen to listen to my thoughts about how I like to play football. Everything felt right".

How did you find your first season with Arsenal?

"I enjoyed being part of the Club from the start. I struck up a great understanding on and off the pitch with Ian Wright and we had some great moments together. I suppose my main memories of that year were my first goal for the Club against Southampton and then my goal in the final match, at home to Bolton, which guaranteed European football for the following year."

The 1997/98 Double-winning season was an incredible year for the Club and you personally. What moments stand out for you?

Dennis scored the last goal of a 4–1 win at Norwich in August 2004

"Of course, lifting the Premiership and FA Cup trophies were the most important. However, my hat-trick against Leicester City will never be forgotten and winning numerous player of the year and goal of the season awards was very touching. I still look back on that year with great affection and probably always will."

How did the 2001/02 Double-winning season compare?

"It was different in that, in 2002, it was about proving that our previous Double had not been a one-off fluke. But there were also so many similar aspects: the way we played our best football and got our best results after Christmas, for instance. It was incredible to secure the Double at Old Trafford and I was delighted to play in the FA Cup final that season, having missed the 1998 final through injury."

You were a key player in the 49-match unbeaten league run. How did that rank among your other achievements at Arsenal?

"It's interesting because during the unbeaten run we won the Premiership title and yet the run gets mentioned more than the championship. Naturally, I am extremely proud of that run and of winning the championship. During the unbeaten run, we didn't pay a great deal of attention to it within the dressing-room. Perhaps as time goes on, it will truly dawn on me what we achieved there."

You have previously said Arsenal is a very special club. Why do you think that?

"Well, I just think the traditions of the Club are there for all to see. The Club has always done things the right way and with a bit of

class. Also, how many other stadiums in the world are as nice as Highbury with the marble halls and so on? And now, when you look at the plans for the new stadium, you can again see that quality and character are at the foreground of it all. I also feel the fans have a special spirit; I am certainly very grateful to them for all the support they've shown me."

FIVE GREAT BERGKAMP GOALS

Arsenal 4–2 Southampton
September 23, 1995

"I scored my first two goals for Arsenal that day. I just remember the reaction of the crowd to my first. It was so touching to notice how pleased for me they were."

Arsenal 1–0 Manchester United
November 4, 1995

"I was one-on-one with Peter Schmeichel but I managed to beat him which was great. My first goal against Manchester United."

Arsenal 3–1 Tottenham Hotspur
November 24, 1996

"Again, the reaction of the fans is key to my memories. The place absolutely erupted and you could see from my celebrations that I shared the fans' joy."

Leicester City 3–3 Arsenal
August 27, 1997

"The final goal of my hat-trick was my favourite. Everything about the finish went exactly as I intended."

Newcastle United 0–2 Arsenal
March 2, 2002

"It's funny but I didn't realise until after I had scored how great this goal looked. As I turned away to celebrate, I noticed from the reactions of my team-mates and the Arsenal fans that it must have been special."

That champion feeling: Dennis with the Premiership trophy in May 2002

Bergkamp is congratulated by the skipper after scoring Arsenal's second against Manchester United at Highbury in 2004–05

21 Years young!

Can you believe it, the Junior Gunners supporters club is now 21 years old! Throughout its existence the Junior Gunners – a supporters club for both boys and girls up to 16 years of age – has evolved and grown. It now boasts members from around the world, including New Zealand, the Middle East, Slovakia, the Fiji Islands, Iceland and Zambia!

We spoke with Junior Gunners membership and travel manager Sue Campbell and she told us about the past, present and future of the Junior Gunners – also how past members are now representing the club on and off the pitch!

How has the Junior Gunners evolved during its first 21 years?
"Well, for a start, membership has risen from 7,000 to 22,000. The Christmas party has gone from seeing just a few members coming along to watch the team train, to full-blown parties with food, games, quizzes, prizes and presents. We have also started taking Junior Gunners to matches abroad! Members stay at youth hostels and sometimes get to meet players during their Champions' League warm-up sessions. I think we've all enjoyed receiving visitors here at Highbury, including guests from Lens FC in France, Lord's Cricket Ground and others. They come along on match day, play some friendly football against our Junior Gunners in our indoor gym, have a meal and then watch the match from the Family Enclosure."

How involved do the players and the manager get with the Junior Gunners?
The players are brilliant. We have access to the whole squad twice a season – once for the Christmas party and then for our awards. They come along and chat to our members, sign autographs and pose for photographs. On match days, Patrick Vieira is brilliant with the mascot and you should see Mr Wenger applaud the mascot as he or she comes off the pitch at kick-off.

What are the main benefits on offer for Junior Gunners members?
"The chance to represent Arsenal Football Club as a matchday mascot! We choose our mascots completely at random from the computer, they all receive a goodie bag, a team photograph, birthday and Christmas cards, newsletters and a chance to enter quizzes and competitions! Some of our brilliant prizes include an invitation to come along to our annual Christmas party, where they can meet the players!"

Are you still in touch with any graduates from the Junior Gunners?
"Yes! Daniel Quy, my assistant manager, was a Junior Gunner himself – in fact he was the first Junior Gunner mascot for the club! There are also many other members of staff who began their Highbury lives as members of the Junior Gunners, including Ashley Cole! When we travel to away matches, we often bump into ex-members. It is really strange when they introduce their children to you who are now members themselves."

Do you foresee the Junior Gunners still going strong in another 21 years?
"Of course, this is where the heart of the club is! This is where you capture your future supporters. As we always say: 'You look after the children, they will bring their parents, and when they are parents, they will bring their children!'"

Lucky Junior Gunners have the chance to meet players, go to the Christmas Party and be the club mascot

To join the Junior Gunners
ring 020 7704 4140 or email
juniorgunners@arsenal.co.uk

ACROSS

1 Arsenal's home for 93 years (8)
4 Senor Fabregas (4)
6 Colour of away shirt in 2003 (6)
8 Hr. Van Persie (5)
9 How fans describe big victory (4)
10 _____ your hearts out for the lads (4)
12 M. Pires (6)
15 Dutch master in attack (6)
18 Goalkeeping hero of the 2005 FA Cup Final (7)
19 What will be home from 2006 (8)

DOWN

1 Top goalscorer in 2004–05 (5)
2 Brazilian midfielder (8)
3 Super Spanish striker (5)
4 England's Arsenal left-back (4)
5 Penalties saved in 2005 FA Cup Final (3)
7 Most successful manager in Highbury history (6)
10 Solid Swiss defender (8)
11 What thinking footballers use (5)
13 Ivory Coast defender M. Toure (4)
14 How fans describe the opposition (4)
16 Goals in Spurs v Arsenal at White Hart Lane in 2004–05 (4)
17 Dependable defender Campbell (3)

Are you a Gunners genius?

See History lesson Q4

Have you been paying attention at the back? Well here is your chance to prove it. Tackle these questions and find out whether or not you are an Arsenal mastermind or the weakest link!

Shooting stars

1 True or false: Both Robin Van Persie and Dennis Bergkamp have played for Ajax.
2 In which capital city was Thierry Henry born?
3 Thierry Henry scored a hat-trick against which south coast Premiership team in March 2005: Portsmouth or Southampton?
4 Who did Robin Van Persie score his first Champions' League goal against?
5 How many goals did Dennis Bergkamp score in Arsenal's 5–4 victory over Tottenham Hotspur at White Hart Lane?
6 What nationality is young Gunner Arturo Lupoli?
7 Which Manchester side did Quincy Owusu-Abeyie make his first-team debut: United or City?
8 Thierry Henry scored his first two goals of the 2004–05 season in a 5–3 home victory against which north east side?
9 Which London side did Jose Antonio Reyes score his first Arsenal goal against?
10 Which striker netted the team's first Premiership goal of the 2004–05 season?

Defence witness

1 Which team did Gael Clichy join Arsenal from?
2 True or false: Kolo Toure has never scored in the UEFA Champions League.
3 Before retiring from international football, which country did Lauren play for?
4 Which Arsenal defender helped Switzerland keep a clean sheet against France in March 2005?
5 Pascal Cygan's number 18 shirt was previously worn by which other Frenchman: Sylvain Wiltord or Gilles Grimandi?
6 Against which team did the Gunners keep their first Premiership clean sheet of 2004–05: Blackburn Rovers or Everton?
7 Which goalkeeper helped Arsenal win their 2005 FA Cup penalty shoot-out against Sheffield United: Jens Lehmann or Manuel Almunia?
8 Kolo Toure and which other Arsenal defender come from the Ivory Coast?
9 Which legendary basketball player inspired Sol Campbell's choice of the number 23 shirt?
10 Who scored the Gunners' winner at Portsmouth in the 2004–05 season?

History lesson

1 What was the first name that Arsenal FC played under?
2 The Gunners have won doubles in 1971, 1998 and which other year?
3 In what year did Arsenal beat Parma to win the European Cup Winners' Cup?
4 Which team did the Gunners beat in both the 1993 FA and League Cup finals?
5 The Gunners won their first league championship in which year: 1899 or 1931?
6 Arsenal beat the same team in the 1950 and 1971 FA Cup Finals. Was it Liverpool or Everton?
7 Which manager led Arsenal to the 1971 double: George Graham or Bertie Mee?
8 Who was the first Japanese player to appear for Arsenal?
9 Which two members of Arsenal's 1998 double-winning squad also captained England?
10 Which other London club did Gunners legend Liam Brady play for?

See Shooting stars Q4

See Middle class Q7 (No 15)

See Coaching staff Q6

Middle class

1. Which Arsenal midfielder is nicknamed Bobby?
2. Which Arsenal player appeared in the 2004 Uefa Cup Final for Marseille.
3. The Diambars football academy in Africa was co-created by which Gunners midfielder?
4. What team did Edu join Arsenal from: Corinthians or AC Milan?
5. Which Arsenal player joined the Club from Swedish club Halmstads?
6. Who scored the winner at St James' Park in the December 2004 Premiership meeting?
7. Cesc Fabregas joined Arsenal from which Spanish giants: Real Madrid or Barcelona?
8. Which Arsenal midfielder scored twice against Aston Villa in October 2004?
9. Who became Arsenal's most capped player when he appeared against Switzerland in March 2005.
10. True or false: Patrick Vieira opened the scoring in the 2004 Community Shield.

Coaching staff

1. Which member of the coaching team has taken part in all three Arsenal doubles as either a player or coach?
2. Arsène Wenger won the 1988 French League championship with which team?
3. In which country did Arsène Wenger win the 1996 Super Cup: China or Japan?
4. True or false: Boro Primorac once captained Yugoslavia as a player?
5. Head Of Youth Development Liam Brady won the FA Cup with Arsenal in what year: 1979 or 1982?
6. In what year did Arsène Wenger join Arsenal?
7. True or false: Steve Bould, under-17s coach, was part of Arsenal's 1998 double-winning squad?
8. What was the name of the team that Arsène Wenger left to join Arsenal?
9. What subject does Arsène Wenger have a degree in: economics or chemistry?
10. True or false: physio Gary Lewin was a striker in Arsenal's youth team.

WORDSEARCH AND SPOT THE BALL

```
F L F A B R E G A S L H B S A
B C O N H L P X F I B E D P S
J H O J P I N E C L K N E O H
P A T K E R W E N G E R L E B
I M B K L T I Y C J N Y Y R U
R P A P I T I O T N E R N O R
E I L J H T J H L N U E O B T
S O L L O L I O W B X U Z I O
N N H U I E L P H E U G I N N
J S R O E L G G K C I A T A G
Q E F L A M I N I J E E S L R
Y D K W V H C O E U L L B M O
N E R U A L K C I R T A P E V
H E L B O U F O R T Y N I N E
J B S E R S R E N N U G X L P
```

Are you a true Arsenal fan? Do you have eagle-eyes? Well here's the place to put yourself to the test! In the grid on the left, we have hidden 20 Arsenal related words. They are listed below, but can you find them?

AFC	LAUREN
ASHBURTON GROVE	LEAGUE
CHAMPIONS	PATRICK
FABREGAS	PIRES
FLAMINI	ROBIN
FOOTBALL	SOL
FORTY-NINE	THREE
GUNNERS	TOURE
HENRY	WENGER
HIGHBURY	WHITE

WHERE DO YOU THINK THE BALL IS – A, B, C OR D?

Keeping Track!

Patrick Vieira says that everyone at Arsenal is determined to improve each season. With the fill-in chart, you can keep track of how Arsenal fares during the 2005–06 season and compare it to the previous season. Enjoy!

FA PREMIERSHIP	SEASON 2004–05	SEASON 2005–06
Final position	Second (behind Chelsea)	
First home win	Middlesbrough 5–3	
First away win	Everton 4–1	
First home draw	Bolton W 2–2	
First away draw	Crystal Palace 1–1	
First home defeat	Man Utd 2–4	
First away defeat	Man Utd 0–2	

DOMESTIC CUPS	SEASON 2004–05	SEASON 2005–06
FA Cup	Winners (beat Man Utd in Final)	
Carling Cup	Round Five: Man Utd 0–1	
Community Shield	Winners beat Man Utd 3–1	

CHAMPIONS LEAGUE	SEASON 2004–05	SEASON 2005–06
Progress	Last 16: Bayern Munich 2–3 agg	
First home win	PSV Eindhoven 1–0	
First away win	None	
First home draw	Panathinaikos 1–1	
First away draw	Rosenborg 1–1	
First home defeat	None	
First away defeat	Bayern Munich 1–3	

GOALS	SEASON 2004–05	SEASON 2005–06
First in Premiership	Dennis Bergkamp v Everton	
First in FA Cup	Jose Antonio Reyes v Stoke (R3)	
First in Carling Cup	Robin Van Persie v Man City (R3)	
First in Champions League	Freddie Ljungberg v Rosenborg	

CLEAN SHEETS	SEASON 2004–05	SEASON 2005–06
First in Premiership	Jens Lehmann v Blackburn (H)	
First in FA Cup	Jens Lehmann v Wolves (R4)	
First in Carling Cup	None	
First in Champions League	Jens Lehmann v PSV Eindhoven	

Arsenal **Answers**

Spot the difference

Here are the 12 differences. Did you get them?

Spot the ball

Answer: B

Arsenal Quiz

Shooting stars
1. False – Robin played for Feyenoord
2. Paris
3. Portsmouth
4. Rosenborg
5. None
6. Italian
7. City
8. Middlesbrough
9. Chelsea
10. Bergkamp

Defence witness
1. Cannes
2. False, he scored against Bayern
3. Cameroon
4. Phillippe Senderos
5. Grimandi
6. Blackburn Rovers
7. Manuel Almunia
8. Emmanuel Eboue
9. Michael Jordan
10. Sol Campbell

History lesson
1. Dial Square
2. 2004
3. 1994
4. Sheffield Wednesday
5. 1931
6. Liverpool
7. Bertie Mee
8. Junichi Inamoto
9. David Platt and Tony Adams
10. West Ham United

Middle class
1. Robert Pires
2. Mathieu Flamini
3. Patrick Vieira
4. Corinthians
5. Freddie Ljungberg
6. Patrick Vieira
7. Barcelona
8. Robert Pires
9. Patrick Vieira
10. False, it was Gilberto

Coaching staff
1. Pat Rice
2. Monaco
3. Japan
4. True
5. 1979
6. 1996
7. True
8. Grampus Eight
9. Economics
10. False, he was a goalkeeper

Wordsearch

F	L	F	A	B	R	E	G	A	S	L	H	B	S	A
B	C	O	N	H	L	P	X	F	I	B	E	D	P	S
J	H	O	J	P	I	N	E	C	L	K	N	E	O	H
P	A	T	K	E	R	W	E	N	G	E	R	L	E	B
I	M	B	K	L	T	I	Y	C	J	N	Y	Y	R	U
R	P	A	P	I	T	I	O	T	N	E	R	N	O	R
E	L	J	H	T	J	H	L	N	U	E	O	B	T	
S	O	L	L	O	L	I	O	W	B	X	U	Z	I	O
N	N	H	U	I	E	L	P	H	E	U	G	I	N	N
J	S	R	O	E	L	G	G	K	C	I	A	T	A	G
Q	E	F	L	A	M	I	N	I	J	E	E	S	L	R
Y	D	K	W	V	H	C	O	E	U	L	L	B	M	O
N	E	R	U	A	L	K	C	I	R	T	A	P	E	V
H	E	L	B	O	U	F	O	R	T	Y	N	I	N	E
J	B	S	E	R	S	R	E	N	N	U	G	X	L	P

Arsenal Crossword

Across
1. Highbury
4. Cesc
6. Yellow
8. Robin
9. Easy
10. Sing
12. Robert
15. Dennis
18. Lehmann
19. Emirates

Down
1. Henry
2. Gilberto
3. Reyes
4. Cole
5. One
6. Wenger
10. Senderos
11. Brain
13. Kolo
14. Them
16. Nine
17. Sol

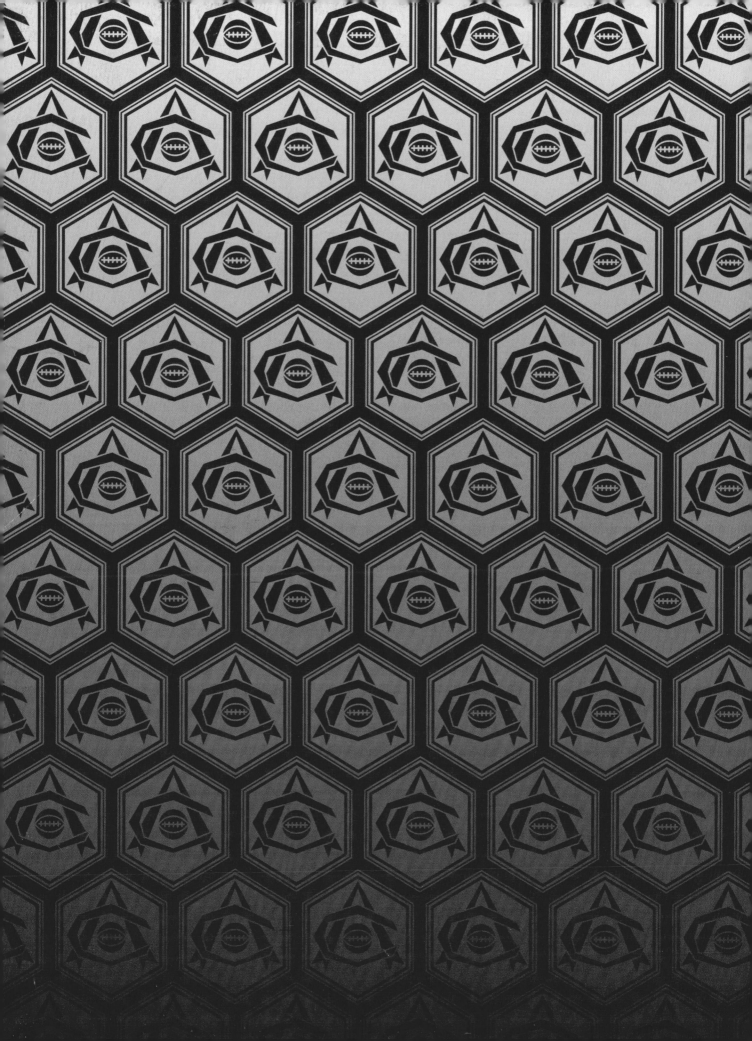